RESOURCE BOOKS FOR TEACHERS

series editor
ALAN MALEY

FILM

Susan Stempleski and Barry Tomalin

OXFORD
UNIVERSITY PRESS

OXFORD
UNIVERSITY PRESS

Great Clarendon Street, Oxford OX2 6DP

Oxford University Press is a department of the University of Oxford. It furthers the University's objective of excellence in research, scholarship, and education by publishing worldwide in

Oxford   New York

Athens   Auckland   Bangkok   Bogotá   Buenos Aires
Cape Town   Chennai   Dar es Salaam   Delhi   Florence
Hong Kong   Istanbul   Karachi   Kolkata   Kuala Lumpur
Madrid   Melbourne   Mexico City   Mumbai   Nairobi   Paris
Sao Paulo   Singapore   Taipei   Tokyo   Toronto   Warsaw

with associated companies in   Berlin   Ibadan

Oxford and Oxford English are registered trade marks of Oxford University Press in the UK and in certain other countries

Photocopying

ISBN 0 19 437231 6

Printed in China

Acknowledgements

The authors gratefully acknowledge the support of their colleagues in Media Special Interest Group of TESOL and the Video Interest Section of TESOL, in particular, Paul Arcario, Joe Hambrook, Ulla Ladau-Harjulin, and Professor Jack Lonergan. They are also very grateful for the support of Alan Maley, Series Editor, and Julia Sallabank, Belinda Fenn, and Bruce Wade at Oxford University Press.

The authors and the publisher are also grateful to those who have given permission to reproduce the following extracts and adaptations of copyright material:

p12 From *The Shawshank Redemption: The Shooting Script*. Compilation and design copyright © 1994 by Castle Rock Entertainment. All rights reserved. Reprinted with permission of Newmarket Press, 18 East 48 Street, New York, NY 10017.

p50 Extract from Annie Hall from *Four Films of Woody Allen*. Copyright © 1977, United Artists Corporation. All rights reserved.

p72 From *Ordinary People* by Judith Guest. Copyright © 1976 by Judith Guest.

p86 'Willis surprises in heartfelt ghost story "The Sixth Sense"' by Margaret A. McGurk, *The Cincinnati Enquirer* 6 August 1999. Used with permission from *The Cincinnati Enquirer*/Margaret A. McGurk.

p90 From *The Joy Luck Club* by Amy Tan. Copyright © 1989 by Amy Tan, first published by Penguin Putnam. Excerpted and reprinted by permission of Amy Tan, Abner Stein, and G.P. Putnam's Sons, a division of Penguin Putnam Inc.

Illustrations by Brian Williamson p64, 65, 74, 75.

The publisher would like to thank the following for permission to reproduce photographs:

The Kobal Collection p28 (Marlene Dietrich/Don English); The Moviestore Collection pp28 (Humphrey Bogart and Lauren Bacall/1946 Warner Bros.), 115 (Judy Garland); The Ronald Grant Archive pp22 (Titanic poster), 48 (The Mask of Zorro).

Contents

Foreword

We live in a culture dominated by the visual image, and in particular, the moving image. The written word has, to a large extent, ceded its pre-eminence to visual representations of the world which in turn has created the need for us to make sense of this visual rhetoric. Moving pictures have a grammar and discourse all their own which we need to decode if we are to understand the meanings that they contain.

In language teaching terms, film offers a wide range of alternatives. It is increasingly available through video, satellite, TV broadcasting, the Internet, and DVD. Film is a medium which is globally accessible, even in environments where technology is not widely available.

Film attracts students through the power it has to tell a story. It contextualises language through the flow of images, making it more accessible. Motivation to engage with a narrative, especially one with a high affective charge, is enhanced. The combination of sound, vision and language engages and stimulates our senses and cognitive faculties simultaneously, creating a total impact that dwarfs other mediums.

Film also offers an enlargement of our knowledge of the world and the cultures that it contains. It is in the broadest sense 'educational'.

But simply to view films in English is not enough. To appreciate them fully and at the same time develop our linguistic powers, help is needed in accessing their messages and in integrating them with language learning. This is precisely what this book offers.

Alan Maley

The authors and series editor

Susan Stempleski teaches at the Hunter College International English Language Institute of the City University of New York and regularly conducts workshops on media-based language teaching at Columbia University Teachers College. Internationally recognized as an expert on the use of video and other technologies in language teaching, she has lectured in more than thirty countries around the world. Her numerous publications include *Video in Second Language Teaching, Cultural Awareness, EarthWatch, Focus on the Environment*, and *Getting Together*. She is Series Editor of the *ABC News Intermediate ESL Video Library*, ESL Director and Supervising Editor of the *Hello, America* multimedia ESL course, and co-author of *That's English!*, a telecourse produced by BBC English and the Spanish Ministry of Education and Science. In addition to her work as a teacher, teacher-trainer, and author, she has been a consultant for such organizations as Children's Television Workshop, Encyclopedia Britannica, Microsoft Corporation, and the World Bank.

Barry Tomalin is visiting lecturer in Media and Technology at the University of Westminster in London and conducts seminars internationally in the use of media and culture in language learning. He is also a film buff. Formerly Editor of BBC English in the BBC World Service, he is an internationally known trainer, writer, and broadcaster who has trained teachers in more than 30 countries worldwide. Among his publications are: *TV, Video and Radio in the English Class, Video in the English Class, Video in Action* and *Cultural Awareness* (both with Susan Stempleski), *Culture Watch*, and *Teaching English with Technology*. Barry is author of the BBC English self-study course *Follow Me*, and Editor and co-author of the Spanish Ministry of Education /BBC co-production *That's English*. He has also produced a primary and secondary English project for Spain. Barry acts as a publishing and cross-cultural consultant for a number of international publishers and corporations.

Alan Maley worked for The British Council from 1962 to 1988, serving as English Language Officer in Yugoslavia, Ghana, Italy, France, and China, and as Regional Representative in South India (Madras). From 1988 to 1993 he was Director-General of the Bell Educational Trust, Cambridge. From 1993 to 1998 he was Senior Fellow in the Department of English Language and

Literature of the National University of Singapore. He is currently a freelance consultant and Director of the graduate programme at Assumption University, Bangkok. Among his publications are *Literature*, in this series, *Beyond Words*, *Sounds Interesting*, *Sounds Intriguing*, *Words*, *Variations on a Theme*, and *Drama Techniques in Language Learning* (all with Alan Duff), *The Mind's Eye* (with Françoise Grellet and Alan Duff), *Learning to Listen* and *Poem into Poem* (with Sandra Moulding), *Short and Sweet*, and *The Language Teacher's Voice*.

Introduction

Who is this book for?

We have written this book for both practising teachers of English as a second or foreign language, and teachers in training. Our aim is to provide a collection of ready-to-use, film-based classroom activities for teachers working with learners at all levels, from elementary to advanced. Although our emphasis is on the teaching of English as a second or foreign language, the activities we describe can easily be adapted to the teaching of other languages.

Why use film?

The value of film as a language teaching and learning resource is self-evident. It is motivating, and it provides a source of authentic and varied language. Many films are well known, and some are recognized worldwide as a common frame of reference. The medium of film is excellent at communicating cultural values, attitudes, and behaviours. It is very effective at bringing the outside world into the classroom and providing a stimulating framework for classroom communication and discussion.

What approach is used?

The activities in this collection look at feature films in three ways.

1 They encourage students to improve their English by watching film, observing what goes on, hearing what is said, and describing what happens in their own words.

2 They motivate students to observe and discuss the techniques of filmmaking itself and to understand how the choice of **shot**, lighting, **editing**, and sound all influence our view of the story being told.

3 A number of activities address the film industry and invite the student to explore the world of film **stars** and publicity and to understand how a film gets made in the first place. An important part of this understanding are the activities which invite students to compare the products of the Hollywood film industry with films made in their own country.

Activities are offered at all levels of proficiency, allowing teachers to progress from simple viewing and language study activities to more sophisticated content study and project work.

This collection of activities focuses primarily on the use of feature films, i.e. commercial films for cinema release, rather than on documentaries, TV dramas, or advertisements, although many of the activities can be adapted for use with these formats. A few activities use film **trailers** as opportunities to study how stories can be summarized in a few seconds and to illustrate the publicity side of the industry. But the story, told with pictures, words, and music, is the most important thing in a film, and this is what we emphasize in most of the activities.

Techniques for using films on video

For more than fifty years teachers have been using films both in and outside the language class, sometimes having students watch a feature film related to a set book for context, sometimes presenting a film on a Friday afternoon for relaxation, and sometimes using short **clips** for language study. A few decades ago the only option for presentation of a film or film clip was straight-through viewing; replays of individual **scenes** and pauses at selected points were impossible. However, the video revolution has changed all this. New technologies such as the videocassette and the digital versatile disc (DVD) allow for much greater versatility in the way films can be shown, and teachers can choose from an ever-widening variety of techniques for presenting and exploiting films in the classroom. In our own experience, videos of feature films can form the basis of an enormous range of dynamic and motivating classroom activities.

The controls on a VCR or DVD player allow a variety of ways of presenting film. Here is a selection of basic video presentation techniques that less-experienced teachers may wish to familiarize themselves with.

Vision on/sound off (silent viewing)

This technique is useful for highlighting visual content, for stimulating student language use about what they see on the screen, and for getting students to guess or predict the language used on the **soundtrack**. Some suggestions include:

- present short scenes where the **setting**, **action**, props, etc. give clues to what is being said on the soundtrack, and get students to guess the actual words spoken by the actors.

- show longer scenes and ask students to suggest the gist of the conversation or to describe the general situation. With lower-level classes, a series of questions like the following can help to focus the discussion: *Who are these people? Where are they? Why are they there? What are they talking about?*
- ask students to produce an oral or written commentary on what they see
- play short scenes and get students to imagine and write appropriate **screenplays**, which can then be compared with the actual **dialogue**.

Sound on/vision off (sound only)

Teachers can use this technique to get students to pay close attention to what they hear on the soundtrack. Students can use what they hear on the soundtrack, i.e. dialogue, **sound effects**, and/or music to make predictions about the setting, the situation, the **characters**, and the action. Some ways of using the sound-only technique include:

- ask students to draw a picture, or series of pictures, of what they expect to see on the screen
- ask students to respond to a series of questions about the scene, for example: *Where are the people? How many people are there in the scene? How are they dressed? What are they doing?*
- ask students to produce an oral or written commentary on what they hear
- ask students to draw up a list of things (people, props, actions, etc.) they expect to see on the screen.

Pause/still/freeze-frame control

Teachers can use this technique to interrupt the action at selected points. Suggestions include:

- pause the video at the beginning of each dialogue and ask the students to predict the line they will hear
- pause at strategic points in the action and ask the students to describe what has happened, or predict what is going to happen
- pause at points where actors use meaningful gestures or facial expressions and ask students to suggest the thoughts and feelings of the characters.

Sound and video on (normal viewing)

Ideas include:

- tell students what the **sequence** will be about and ask them to make a list of all the things they expect to see and hear on the video
- give students a list of comprehension questions before viewing a sequence and then get them to answer the questions after viewing
- ask the students to produce an oral or written summary of what they saw and heard on the video
- give the students a **transcript** of a sequence and ask them to practise acting it out before viewing the actual sequence. After viewing they can compare and discuss the different performances.

Split viewing

In this technique, some students, the 'viewers', see a video sequence but do not hear the soundtrack; others, the 'listeners', hear the soundtrack but do not see the video. Teachers use this technique as the basis for a variety of information gap procedures, for example:

- viewers describe what they have seen to listeners, and listeners describe what they have heard to viewers
- viewers and listeners work together to reconstruct the whole sequence from the elements they have separately seen and heard
- listeners ask viewers questions about the scene and reconstruct it from the viewers' answers and from what they themselves have heard on the soundtrack.

Jumbled sequence

Teachers divide a sequence into sections and play them out of order. This technique is useful for stimulating discussion and getting students to focus on editing techniques and the actual storyline in a sequence:

- show the beginning and end of a sequence and ask students to guess what happens in the middle
- show a number of sequences out of programme order and ask students to order them

- choose two short sequences each from three different films and show them in random order; students must allocate the sequences to the films and decide on the order of the sequences in each film.

Recent technological advances

Two major technological developments in recent years have been the introduction of DVDs (digital versatile discs) and the Internet. Enormous amounts of film information are now available on the Internet, and films on videocassette or in DVD format can be ordered through the Internet. It is still important to remember, both for videocassettes and DVDs, that television standards vary from country to country, and you need to order the correct format for your country. We have included a list of TV standards (PAL, NTSC, or SECAM) around the world in Appendix D, 'International TV standards for video', on page 151, and a list of DVD regions and the geographical areas they cover in Appendix E, 'DVD worldwide regions', on page 154.

DVD is a new and growing resource of film material that is of equal interest to the language teacher and the media studies teacher. In addition to the film itself, some DVDs contain examples of **theatrical trailers**, as well as **subtitles** or captions in one or more languages. Many DVDs include documentaries about the **director**, the actors, or the making of the film, and some include a version of the film with **voice-over** comments by the director or **producer**. These features can be immensely valuable to the teacher interested in looking at film as content and in focusing on the thinking behind and the process of making a film. Activities for exploiting many of these features are included in this book. In conjunction with this, you will also find a helpful list of film technical terms in Appendix A, 'Glossary of film terms', on page 141.

It is likely that DVD will supersede video in a short time, but a word of warning to teachers. Although DVDs have advantages in picture, sound, and still photograph quality, you cannot wind through and pause a DVD at exactly the point you want as you currently can with a videocassette. DVDs lack this aspect of classroom flexibility. For this reason you may wish to keep your most popular films for use in class in both formats. Another practical point to bear in mind is that schools that have invested in video players may not wish to re-invest quickly in DVD players.

How to use this book

How the book is organized

Film is divided into seven chapters:

Chapter 1, **About film**, brings together activities that focus on discussion of film and the film industry in general and are not tied into the viewing of any particular film material.

Chapter 2, **Working with film clips**, presents ideas for involving students in viewing, analysing and discussing film clips.

Chapter 3, **Creating film-related materials**, includes activities in which students produce film-related materials such as film **treatments**, **storyboards**, and **scripts**.

Chapter 4, **Responding to whole films**, describes activities in which students reflect, write about, and discuss whole films they have seen.

Chapter 5, **Making comparisons**, outlines activities in which students compare different elements of film, versions of films, or film-related materials.

Chapter 6, **Focusing on characters**, concentrates on activities in which the students are involved in analysing, discussing, or writing about film characters.

Chapter 7, **Project work**, presents descriptions of film-related projects which engage learners over a period of time, and outlines ways in which activities in other chapters of the book can be grouped to produce a variety of coherently organized projects.

In addition to the activities there are six appendices, including a glossary of film terms, a list of film-related websites, a video troubleshooting guide, and a bibliography. Other appendices provide useful information on international TV standards and worldwide DVD regions.

Using films successfully

In our view, there are three keys to the successful use of films in the classroom: film selection, activity choice, and implementation.

Film selection

In our experience teachers tend to approach the use of film in four ways:

- from the film itself—This is a terrific film! How can I use it?
- from the language to be taught or reinforced—Here's a great sequence using the present perfect!
- more rarely, from the point of view as film as culture—This scene really shows how people think!
- technique—I can get my class to analyse how this sequence was put together.

All these approaches are valid but a few selection guidelines may be in order.

1 In limited class periods, short film clips of two to five minutes are going to be more useful than longer sequences.

2 You will need to think about playing your clip at least three times in the class period—once for general comprehension, once for more detailed study, and once for discussion. However, the number of times you play the film clip will depend partly on the activity you choose, as well as elements such as the density and level of language on the soundtrack.

3 You need to be aware of copyright restrictions on video. These restrictions vary from country to country so it is important to know: (a) the copyright laws in your own country, and (b) the restrictions on the use of the videocassette or DVD that you wish to use.

If in doubt, you can always contact the film or video distributor for your country and enquire about the conditions for educational use.

Film logs

As different teachers use the activities in this book they will discover different films or film clips that work successfully in class, or they will find the activities can be adapted easily to film clips they already use. To facilitate this process many teachers find it useful to keep a film log in the staff room. Teachers can use the log to write up the **titles** and details of films or film clips they have used with particular activities, and other teachers can consult the log. In this way knowledge about particular films and activities is easily and usefully shared.

A typical entry in a film log looks like this:

Title	Description	Activity in *Film*	Time / level
Sabrina Fair (1954) Sabrina (1995)	*Scene where elder brother calls younger brother for chat with their father. Ends with younger brother sitting on champagne glasses.*	*5.1 Original vs. remake*	*40–50 minutes/ Intermediate and above*

Activity choice

Many activities contain extensions and variations that demonstrate how the activities can be adapted to different levels or extended to make longer lessons.

Several activities contain worksheets that can be photocopied and distributed to students or used as models for new activities that you might wish to produce. In some cases we suggest appropriate films for the activities, and there are some activities that do not require the film at all and can be done independently of the visual input.

How each activity in this book is organized

To facilitate activity choice, we provide a brief summary of what the students do in the activity and the following information:

Level	the minimum proficiency level at which the activity can be carried out. Sometimes a range of levels is suggested to show that, with suitable modifications, the activity can be used at different levels.
Time	a rough guide to the amount of time it will take to do the activity in class.
Materials	a list of any special materials you will need to do the activity.
Preparation	a description of what preparation you need to do before the activity.
Procedure	step-by-step instructions for carrying out the activity in class.
Variations	for some activities we describe ways that you can modify the activity for different proficiency levels, for different types of material, or to practise different language skills.

Remarks	we sometimes add comments that we think will be useful to teachers who use the activity.
Photocopiable	for some activities we provide worksheets, survey forms, or other *materials* handouts that you can photocopy and use to do the activity.
Work samples	in a few cases we provide examples of completed diagrams, posters, etc. that are part of the activity.

Implementation

Having decided which film and activity you are going to use, the next and most important step is to implement the lesson. The detailed notes in the *Preparation* section of each activity, together with the instructions in the *Procedure* section, provide step-by-step guidance on how most successfully to carry out film-based activities in the classroom.

A final note

This collection of activities focuses primarily on feature films. As teachers, our prime concern is language information and language development; however, when selecting films and implementing tasks we must never forget that the prime reasons for watching film are entertainment and wonder, which provide the motivation for watching a film clip over and over again. We must be careful to preserve the delicate balance between appreciating a film more because we understand the language, the culture, and the technique behind it, and killing the magic of the experience because we overdo the grammar, the vocabulary, or the pronunciation in the language and comprehension process; or we may simply play the clip too many times or spend too much time in exhaustive linguistic exploitation. One of our prime aims in training teachers is to enhance the appreciation of film while giving teachers and students tools to access it in English. We hope we have achieved that in this book.

1 About film

This section contains 11 lesson plans, all dealing with film from the point of view of the film industry and the audience. None of these activities require the use of the video in the classroom, and all can be done as straight classroom activities. All that is required is that the students enjoy watching films, either in the cinema or on TV or video.

Films are almost as much a topic of conversation as the weather or sports activities, and the activities in this chapter allow students to explore and discuss their favourite films. 'Best film survey' (1.2), 'Favourite films' (1.4), and 'Film brainstorm' (1.5) draw on students' background knowledge and cultural preferences to stimulate group work, conversation, and writing.

'Film trivia quiz' (1.8) and 'Famous film lines' (1.3) offer individual or team quizzes, and activities such as 'Film identity cards' (1.6), 'Film posters' (1.7), 'Oscar ceremony' (1.9), 'Lights!' (1.10), and 'Typecast' (1.11) encourage students to think about different aspects of the film industry. These include film publicity, film stars, and film lighting.

As in all the activities in the book, we try to raise awareness, not just of individual films and film clips, but also of the film industry as a whole. In this respect, we focus on the content of the film industry as subject matter for discussion, as well as on the language used for discussing it. We try to raise critical awareness of film and the film industry and its role in our lives. We work to build a critical awareness of the role of media, and also to practise the four language skills.

1.1 Analysing film scripts

Students analyse an extract from a film script, and make a list of the scriptwriting conventions, such as having the characters' names in capitals, that they find.

LEVEL	**Intermediate and above**
TIME	**15–25 minutes**
MATERIALS	An extract from a film script that has most of these typical scriptwriting conventions (see the sample extract below).

For details of the conventions see *Procedure*.

PREPARATION   Make enough copies of the script to give one to each group of 3–4 students.

PROCEDURE   1 Divide the class into groups of three or four and give one copy of the script to each group. Ask them how it is different from the text in a novel or a newspaper article. Note these points:

- a description of the setting is given at the beginning of each scene
- each scene is numbered
- a new scene number is given for every new setting
- abbreviations are used in setting descriptions, for example 'INT' for *interior*
- capital letters are used for setting locations and times
- the names of characters are: in capital letters
                                        in the centre of the page
                                        on separate lines from the text
- dialogue is centred on the page
- there are no quotation marks around lines of dialogue
- stage directions are: in brackets
                                in the present tense
                                are on separate lines from the dialogue.

2 Tell the class that the script is a few scenes from a film, and then explain the task. Tell them to read the script together in their groups and note down any scriptwriting conventions they notice. It may be useful to provide an example, such as the names of the characters are written in capital letters.

3 Allow students 10–15 minutes to read the script and to take notes.

4 When students have finished reading the script, ask the class what conventions they noticed. Take notes of student answers on the board.

5 Point out any scriptwriting conventions the students may have missed. You may wish to distribute copies of the *Scriptwriting checklist* provided in 3.9, 'Writing film scripts', on page 76, and ask students to compare it with what they noticed.

REMARKS   This activity is a good lead-in to 3.9, 'Writing film scripts', on page 76.

From *The Shawshank Redemption*

9   AN IRON-BARRED DOOR

[slides open with an enormous CLANG. A stark room waits beyond.
CAMERA PUSHES through. SEVEN HUMORLESS MEN sit side by
side at a long table. An empty chair faces them. We are now in:]

INT – SHAWSHANK HEARINGS ROOM – DAY (1947)

[RED enters, removes his cap and waits by the chair.]

                    MAN #1
                     Sit.

[Red sits, tries not to slouch. The chair is uncomfortable.]

                          MAN #2
                We see by your file you've served twenty years of a
                life sentence.

                          MAN #3
                You feel you've been rehabilitated?

                          RED
                Yes, sir. Absolutely. I've learned my lesson. I can
                honestly say I'm a changed man. I'm no longer a
                danger to society. That's the God's honest truth. No
                doubt about it.

[The men just stare at him. One stifles a yawn.]

CLOSEUP – PAROLE FORM

[A big rubber stamp slams down: "REJECTED" in red ink.]

10   EXT – EXERCISE YARD – SHAWSHANK PRISON – DUSK
(1947)

[High stone walls topped with snaky concertina wire, set off at intervals
by looming guard towers. Over a hundred CONS are in the yard.
Playing catch, shooting craps, jawing at each other, making deals.
Exercise period.

Red emerges into fading daylight, slouches low-key through the
activity, worn cap on his head, exchanging hellos and doing minor
business. He's an important man here.]

                          RED (V.O.)
                There's a con like me in every prison in America, I
                guess. I'm the guy who can get it for you. Cigarettes, a
                bag of reefer if you're partial, a bottle of brandy to
                celebrate your kid's high school graduation. Damn
                near anything, within reason.

[He slips somebody a pack of smokes, smooth sleight-of-hand.]

RED (V.O.)
Yes sir, I'm a regular Sears & Roebuck.

The Shawshank Redemption: the Shooting Script. Screenplay by Frank Darabont.
Newmarket Press, New York.

1.2 Best film survey

**Students interview five other students and fill out a form
about the best film they have ever seen.**

LEVEL

Elementary and above

TIME

30–45 minutes

MATERIALS

A survey form for each student (see worksheet below).

PREPARATION

Make enough copies of the survey form to give one to each
student.

PROCEDURE

1 Distribute the survey form. Explain the task to the class. They
should walk around the room and use the form to interview
five different students. Tell them to ask questions to find out
what the different students think is the best film they have
seen, and why. Model the questions and go through the boxes
and words on the form, if necessary.

2 Students walk around the room, interviewing other students
and writing the information in the boxes on the form.

3 When students have completed their interviews, ask for
volunteers to read some of the most interesting answers to the
class.

VARIATION

Instead of, or in addition to, asking about the best film people
have seen, students can interview one another about what they
consider the *worst* film they have seen.

FOLLOW-UP

You can collect the survey forms and display them on the wall for
students to read, and for you to use to gather information about
your students' film preferences.

REMARKS

This activity is a good lead-in to exercises that involve writing film
reviews. (See 4.5, 'Writing film reviews', on page 84.)

BEST FILM SURVEY		
What's the best film you have ever seen?		
Student's name	Film	Reasons
1		
2		
3		
4		
5		

1.3 Famous film lines

Students match famous lines of film dialogue with the names of the actors who spoke them.

LEVEL

Elementary and above

TIME

20–30 minutes

MATERIALS

A worksheet for each group of students (see below).

PREPARATION

Make enough copies of the worksheet to give one to each group of 3–4 students. You could make your own, with lines of recent films that students may be more familiar with.

PROCEDURE

1 Divide the class into groups of three or four and give one worksheet to each group.

2 Explain the task to the students. They should work together in their groups, studying the worksheet and matching each line with the name of the actor or actress who said it, and the film it comes from.

3 When groups have completed the task, get students to take turns reporting the answers.

4 Finish the activity by asking for volunteers to respond to the following questions:

- *What's your favourite film line?*
- *What film is it from?*
- *What's the name of the actor who says the line?*

VARIATION 1

As a writing activity, students at intermediate level and above can write a short report entitled 'My favourite film line'. To guide students in their writing, you can write the the questions above, and also the following questions, on the board or a worksheet:

- *What is the name of the character that says the line?*
- *What is happening at the time the line is spoken?*

VARIATION 2

Students working in pairs or small groups can make their own worksheets with a different set of film lines. Pairs and groups can then quiz each other by exchanging worksheets.

VARIATION 3

With advanced students, distribute a worksheet with incomplete versions of famous film lines, for example, 'May the force … (be with you)' from *Star Wars*. Students work in pairs or groups to finish the line.

REMARKS

This activity is a good lead-in to roleplaying exercises based on famous film scenes. (See 2.11, 'Roleplaying great scenes', on page 49.)

A good source of famous film lines is *Greatest Quotes from Great Films*: http://www.filmsite.org/moments0.html

Acknowledgement

This activity is an adaptation of one presented by Lisa Brickell and Jim Kahny at the Language Institute of Japan International Workshop for Teachers of English in August 1998.

ANSWER KEY

1 f, 2 i, 3 h, 4 e, 5 a, 6 g, 7 j, 8 d, 9 b, 10 c

WORKSHEET

FAMOUS FILM LINES

Do you know these famous film lines? Match each line with the name of the actor who said it and the name of the film it comes from.

Question	Answer
1 'Play it, Sam. Play *As Time Goes By*.'	
2 'May the force be with you.'	
3 'I see dead people.'	
4 'As God is my witness, I'll never be hungry again!'	
5 'We'll make him an offer he can't refuse.'	
6 'Hasta la vista, Baby.'	
7 'Mama always said, "Life is like a box of chocolates."'	
8 'The rain in Spain stays mainly in the plain.'	
9 '… Bond. James Bond.'	
10 'I'm the king of the world!'	

a Marlon Brando in *The Godfather*

b Sean Connery in *Dr. No*

c Leonardo DiCaprio in *Titanic*

d Audrey Hepburn and Rex Harrison in *My Fair Lady*

e Vivien Leigh in *Gone with the Wind*

f Ingrid Bergman in *Casablanca*

g Arnold Schwarzenegger in *Terminator 2: Judgment Day*

h Haley Joe Osment in *The Sixth Sense*

i Harrison Ford in *Star Wars*

j Tom Hanks in *Forrest Gump*

1.4 Favourite films

Students make a list of their ten favourite films, then compare and discuss their lists.

TIME	**Elementary and above**
LEVEL	**20–30 minutes**
MATERIALS	None

PROCEDURE

1 Ask the students to take out a sheet of paper and write down the names of their ten all-time favourite films. Explain to the class that they should not limit their choices to recent films, or films in any particular language—any film is fine.

2 Allow students about five minutes to compile their lists.

3 Divide the class into groups of three or four. Group members compare their lists and discuss these questions:

- *Why are the films on your list your favourites?*
- *What do you especially like about the films?*

4 Ask the students to choose three favourites from their list.

5 Conduct a survey of the class favourites. Students take turns reading the titles of their three favourite films. Each time a different film is mentioned, write the title on the board. Note how many times films are repeated. Create a list of the top ten class favourites and look at the most popular in the class.

6 A list of the results of the class survey can be put on the wall.

FOLLOW-UP

As a follow-up or homework assignment, students could write a composition about their favourite film, answering key questions such as:

- *What is the name of your all-time favourite film?*
- *When and where did you first see the film?*
- *How many times have you seen the film?*
- *What is the film about?*
- *Who are the main actors in the film, and what characters do they play?*
- *What do you especially like about the film?*

VARIATION 1

Ask the students to work in groups and make a list of the group's ten favourite films. Groups then get together to compare and discuss their lists.

VARIATION 2

Ask the students to compare their list of class favourites to published lists of top-grossing British and American films. Such lists are published in British and American film magazines, as well as at these Websites:

The Movie Times: Top 100 Films Ever Worldwide
http://www.the-movie-times.com/thrs.dir/top100world.html

Movie Web: Top 50 All Time Highest Grossing Films
http://www.movieweb.com/movie/alltime.html

Scott Renshaw: 100 Top Grossing Films of All Time
http://inconnect.com/~renshaw/topgross.html

VARIATION 3

Instead of making a list of their favourite films, students, individually or in groups, can make lists of their favourite actors and actresses and then compare and discuss their lists with other students. Appropriate discussion questions about actors on the lists include:

- *Why is he/she one of your favourites?*
- *What films have you seen him/her in?*
- *What's the best film you've seen him/her in?*
- *What do you especially like about him/her?*

REMARKS

For students at intermediate level and above, this activity is a good lead-in to a discussion of the **literary elements** of film. (See 2.13, 'Talk about the story', on page 54.)

1.5 Film brainstorm

Students brainstorm vocabulary related to the film business.

LEVEL

Intermediate and above

TIME

30 minutes

MATERIALS

Sample chart - see below.

PROCEDURE

1 Draw a circle on the board and write the word *film* in the middle of the circle.

2 Divide the class into groups of three or four.

3 Ask each group to say and write as many English words they can think of to do with film.

4 Elicit the words from the class and write them on the board.

5 Now elicit from the class different areas of the film business. Examples might be: *stars, production, distribution, studios, publicity, critics.* Draw a chart on the board, with the name of one of the areas heading each column (see sample chart).

6 Each group takes the words on the board and fits them into the categories. For example, if the words on the board were *studio system*, *scriptwriting*, *agent*, and *trailers*, you might present them like this:

Stars	Production	Distribution	Studios	Publicity	Critics
agent	scriptwriting		studio system	trailers	

Each group can add extra words to each category if they wish, and some words may fit into more than one category.

7 Each group reads out its words and explains them. They explain why they have put the words in particular categories.

8 The categories can be written up as columns and presented on the class noticeboard for reference and addition (see the sample chart).

SAMPLE CHART					
Stars	Production	Distribution	Studios	Publicity	Critics
film star	script-writing	cinema	Hollywood	trailers	reviews
actor	editing	box office	studio system	premiere	Variety
actress	directing	audience	MGM	film	Pauline Kael
	casting	tickets			

Photocopiable © Oxford University Press

1.6 Film identity cards

Students complete identity cards with information about their favourite films, actors, and so on, and then share and discuss the information on the cards with other students.

LEVEL   **Elementary and above**

TIME   **10–15 minutes**

MATERIALS   15 × 10cm file cards or pieces of paper; pins or masking tape; a CD or audiocassette of pleasant background music; a CD or audiocassette player. Sample identity card (see below).

PREPARATION   Make sure you have enough cards and pins for all the students in the class; cue the CD or the audiocassette.

PROCEDURE

1 Give each student a card and a pin or a piece of masking tape.

2 Tell the students to fill out their cards with the following information, making letters large enough to be read by others:
- their first name in the middle
- their favourite **genre** of film in the upper left-hand corner
- the name of a favourite film in the upper right-hand corner
- the name of a favourite female actor in the lower left-hand corner
- the name of a favourite male actor in the lower right-hand corner.

3 Instruct the students to pin or tape their cards onto their clothes. Explain that you will play some music and they should walk around and read the cards of other students. When the music stops, they should take a partner they do not know and ask a question about the information on their card.
- *Who's your favourite film star?*
- *What kind of films do you like?*

Or at higher levels:
- *Why do you like horror films?*
- *What's (name of favourite film star's) best film?*

4 Play the music for about a minute, then stop and give students a chance to choose partners and speak about the information on their cards.

5 Start the music again when you see that most pairs have asked a question and got an answer. Repeat steps 4 and 5 until each student has had a chance to speak to about six partners.

FOLLOW-UP

You can ask students to recall the items on different people's cards: *What's Mario's favourite film? What kind of films does Nina like? Who is Ahmed's favourite actress?*

VARIATION

Read and respond: Each student mentions something that is on a partner's card, and adds a response, for example:

Comment: *Akiko, your favourite actor is Tom Cruise.*
Response: *He's my favourite actor too.*

REMARKS

The students can continue wearing the cards for the remainder of the lesson or even for the next few class meetings, as an aid to learning one another's names.

Acknowledgement

This activity is an adaptation of Gertrude Moskowitz's 'Identity Cards' in *Caring and Sharing in the Language Class* (Rowley, MA: Newbury House Publishers, 1978), pages 46–48.

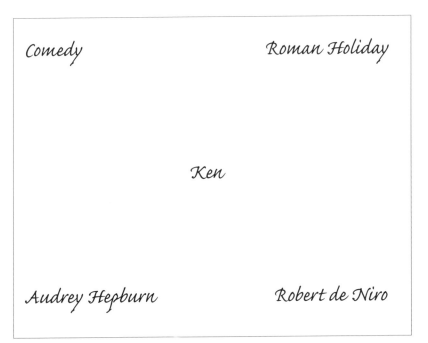

1.7 Film posters

Students examine and discuss film posters.

LEVEL

Elementary and above

TIME

15–20 minutes

MATERIALS

An illustration of a film poster or, if possible, an actual film poster (see below).

PREPARATION

Make enough copies of the poster illustration to give one to each group of 3–4 students. Prepare a brief oral summary of the film that is advertised in the poster. If students haven't seen the film, the summary is particularly important—it will help students decide if the picture and the **strap line** are appropriate (see step 6). An example of a poster you might use is one for *Superman: The Movie* with the strap line 'You'll believe a man can fly!'.

PROCEDURE

1 Preteach or revise the following words:
   - *title* of the film, for example, *Superman: The Movie*
   - *stars*, for example, Christopher Reeve
   - *director*, for example, Richard Lester
   - *strap line* (the advertising line underneath the title), for example, 'You'll believe a man can fly!'
   - *picture*.

2 Elicit from the students the kinds of information they would expect to see on a film poster. Teach any related information you wish.

3 Divide the class into groups of three or four and give one copy of the poster illustration to each group, or display the actual poster in front of the class.

4 Explain the task to the class. The groups should discuss the poster. Tell them to find the film title, the stars, and the director, and describe the picture used to advertise the film.

5 Elicit ideas about the poster.

6 If necessary, give a brief oral summary of the film and check that the students understand it. Ask the class:

- *Does the poster reflect the summary? If not, why not?*
- *Does the strap line reflect the summary? If not, why not?*
- *Can you make any suggestions that will improve the poster?*

FOLLOW-UP   Get the students to design their own film posters.

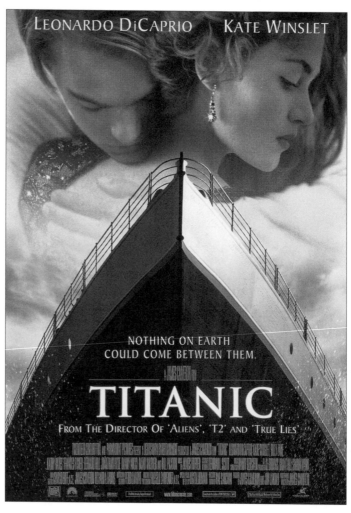

1.8 Film trivia quiz

Students create quizzes about film trivia.

LEVEL

Elementary and above

TIME

Three lessons: 15 minutes in the first lesson, 30–60 minutes in the second, and a follow-up of 30–40 minutes for the quiz.

MATERIALS

Books or magazines about film; worksheets (see below). Depending on the class level, the materials may be in English or in the students' first language.

PREPARATION

Bring in enough film books or magazines for all the students to have a look at; make enough copies of the quiz to give one to each student.

PROCEDURE

Lesson 1

1 Show the students the books and magazines and ask them what sort of information they will find in them (information about films, film stars, etc).

2 Put the class into groups of three or four. Explain the task. Students should use the books to do research at home or in the library, and write some quiz questions for the other groups. Each student should produce five to ten questions, depending on the level of the class. Give some examples, and write them on the board if necessary, for example: *What was the name of the film in which Gene Kelly sang a song called* 'Singin' in the Rain'? (*Singin' in the Rain*).

Lesson 2

3 The students bring their questions to the lesson.

4 Hand out worksheets. Explain to the class that each group should use one sheet of paper to make a question sheet. They should write their questions in English on one side and the answers on the other.

5 Go round each group and help them with vocabulary and grammar. At the end of the session each group should have a sheet of questions and answers.

Lesson 3

6 Appoint a scorer. You are the chairperson. Announce the Film Trivia Quiz and explain that:

- each group must ask a question in turn
- only one member of another group can answer

- there are two points per answer: one point for knowledge and one for expression
- after 30 seconds of silence say *Time's up* and pass the question to another group to answer.

7 The class play the game.

8 At the end of the game, the scorer adds up the scores and announces the winner.

WORKSHEET

FILM TRIVIA QUIZ	
Question	**Answer**
1	*Singin' in the Rain*
2	
3	
4	
5	
6	
7	
8	
9	
10	
11	
12	
13	
14	
15	
16	
17	
18	
19	
20	

1.9 Oscar ceremony

Students choose film stars to present awards at the Oscar ceremony.

LEVEL

Intermediate and above

TIME

30–60 minutes

MATERIALS

A list of current film stars and directors (see below). Refer to Anthony Holden *The Oscars, the Secret History of Hollywood's Academy Awards* (Warner Books, 1994), or http://www.oscar.com, a web site that lists past Oscar winners, and an Academy Award database where you can search for any nominee and get their Oscar history.

PREPARATION

For the *Variation* section, make lists of current film stars and directors or use the sample lists; make enough copies to give one copy of each list to each group of four students.

PROCEDURE

1 Explain the term **A-list**. Check that students understand the meaning of **director**. An **A-list star** or director is one whose name on a new film guarantees a large number of people will come to see the film when it opens. For example, film stars Keanu Reeves or Gwyneth Paltrow, or director Ridley Scott.

2 Divide the class into groups of four.

3 Explain the task. Each group runs a Hollywood studio. They must choose five A-list male stars, five A-list female stars, and one A-list director to present awards at the Oscar ceremony. If necessary, explain the term **Oscar ceremony** (sometimes referred to as *The Oscars*), the annual **Academy Awards** ceremony held in Los Angeles, California.

4 Each 'studio' discusses the lists and chooses its ten stars and one director.

5 Each 'studio' presents its stars and director to the class and explains the reasons for its choices. Encourage students to use phrases like, 'We want to invite 'X' because … . In our opinion her best film is … .'

VARIATION

The class can also nominate and vote on their ten 'all time' A-list film stars for their 'Hall of Fame'.

Here is a personal list of top ten stars.

My all time 'Top Ten' stars list

Men	Women
1 Cary Grant	1 Lauren Bacall
2 Charlie Chaplin	2 Greta Garbo
3 Clark Gable	3 Elizabeth Taylor
4 Harrison Ford	4 Ava Gardner
5 Humphrey Bogart	5 Gwyneth Paltrow
6 Fred Astaire	6 Joan Crawford
7 John Wayne	7 Ginger Rogers
8 Marlon Brando	8 Whoopi Goldberg
9 Jack Nicholson	9 Katharine Hepburn
10 Denzel Washington	10 Michelle Pfeiffer

My favourite film directors

Directors	Most famous film
1 Steven Spielberg (USA)	1 *Jaws*
2 George Lucas (USA)	2 *Star Wars*
3 D.W. Griffiths (USA)	3 *Birth of a Nation*
4 Ingmar Bergman (Sweden)	4 *The Seventh Seal*
5 Akira Kurosawa (Japan)	5 *The Seven Samurai*
6 Woody Allen (USA)	6 *Annie Hall*
7 Sergei Eisenstein (Russia)	7 *Battleship Potemkin*
8 Alfred Hitchcock (Britain)	8 *North by Northwest*
9 François Truffaut (France)	9 *Jules et Jim*
10 Jane Campion (Australia)	10 *The Piano*

1.10 Lights!

Students use film stills (single photographs from a film) to analyse lighting effects.

LEVEL	**Intermediate and above**
TIME	**30 minutes**
MATERIALS	Film **stills** from magazines or books, or use the stills illustrated below.
PREPARATION	Photocopy the film stills as accurately as you can, in order to maintain the distinction of light and shade. Make enough copies to give one to each pair or small group of students.
PROCEDURE	1 Explain the task to the class. The students must describe each still and then decide what effect the lighting has on the **mood** and on the atmosphere of the scene.

1 Explain the task to the class. The students must describe each still and then decide what effect the lighting has on the **mood** and on the atmosphere of the scene.

2 Put the class into pairs or groups and give out the stills.

3 The students describe the scene.

4 Elicit the descriptions from the class.

5 Ask the class to discuss:
   - what kind of film it is
   - what words they would use to express the mood of the scene.

6 Elicit the information from the class and write the words on the board. Make sure everyone understands the words.

7 Ask each group or pair to examine the lighting in the stills.
   - *Whose faces are lit and whose are dark?*
   - *Which parts of the faces or the scenes are lit and which are dark?*
   - *Is there a lot of shadow or a little shadow?*
   - *Is the colour or shade of the scene hard or soft?*
   - *How has the lighting of the scene contributed towards the atmosphere of the film?*

Elicit the answers and discuss with the class.

1.11 Type cast

Students match names of film stars to film publicity.

LEVEL	**Intermediate and above**
TIME	**15–20 minutes**
MATERIALS	Publicity sheets advertising films, with the name of the star removed (see below).
PREPARATION	Make enough copies of the publicity sheets to give one set to each pair or small group of students. Add other stars' names and publicity sheets, if you wish.
PROCEDURE	1 Put the names of 2–3 well-known film stars on the board, and ask the class:

   - *What type of films are these film stars associated with?*
   - *What would you expect to see the film star do in these films?*

2 Divide the class into pairs or small groups. Distribute the copies of the publicity sheets and explain the task to the students. They have to work in their groups, reading the publicity sheets and identifying the stars described in the film publicity.

3 Students work in pairs or small groups to complete the task.

4 Elicit answers from the class.

5 Ask what words and phrases helped them identify the stars.

6 Elicit from the class examples of other 'type cast' stars and the kinds of films the stars appear in.

PUBLICITY SHEET **Name** **Age** born 1930 **Physical type** Tall, dark American actor with soft speech and a slow smile **Dramatic type** – Leading man – Oscar nominated best actor – Started in TV westerns, stars in westerns and 'tough-guy' detective roles	**PUBLICITY SHEET** **Name** **Age** born 1962 **Physical type** American actor, medium build, thick dark hair, lively charismatic style. **Dramatic type** – Leading man – Dynamic, action hero type – Action roles but also capable of sensitive roles (Vietnam paraplegic)
PUBLICITY SHEET **Name** **Age** Born 1967 **Physical type** American, all, attractive, dark haired actress with a large mouth. **Dramatic type** – Romantic comedy or dramatic heroine. – Plays women taking responsibility for their own lives – Oscar nominated – Acted with Hugh Grant in top British comedy	**PUBLICITY SHEET** **Name** **Age** Born 1972 **Physical type** American tall, slim, blonde, very fair, long haired, blue eyes **Dramatic type** – Romantic-comedy roles – Oscar nominated best actress – Plays modern and costume drama roles (Shakespeare)
PUBLICITY SHEET **Name** **Age** born 1968 **Physical type** – Black American, tall, slim, lively, fast talking. – Dramatic type – Singer, dancer and leading man – Comedy and dramatic roles	**PUBLICITY SHEET** **Name** **Age** Born 1964 **Physical type** – French, dark haired actress, medium height, brown eyes, cool beauty – Dramatic type – Dramatic roles in French and International Hollywood roles

2 Working with film clips

These 16 activities involve the use of video and the study of individual film **clips**. In this chapter, the focus moves from the broad view of the industry to the study of the effects and language of specific films. Many of the activities contain worksheets, and all contain descriptions of appropriate types of film clip.

A number of activities focus on the director's intentions in making the film, and invite the students to analyse the director's aims and compare them with their own perceptions. These activities also exploit the growing tendency of 'collector's edition' videocassettes and DVDs to include special features such as theatrical trailers for the featured film, interviews with the director, and voiceover commentary tracks with the director, screenwriter, and producer. Examples of these activities include 'Analysing trailers' (2.1), 'Director's comments' (2.3), and 'Listen to the music' (2.7).

Activities such as 'Complete the timeline' (2.2), 'Eyewitness' (2.4), and 'The memory game' (2.8) focus on students' perceptions of a scene and encourage them to observe and analyse what happens in a film sequence. Other activities, such as 'Hidden meanings' (2.5), 'Images and sounds' (2.6), and 'Point of view' (2.10), encourage students to give their own reactions to what they have seen and heard. Active involvement is required in 'On the phone' (2.9), 'Roleplaying great scenes' (2.12), and 'Show your emotions' (2.13), where students have the opportunity to observe, analyse, and play the **roles** of the actors themselves.

A quiz element is provided by activities such as 'Predict the opening scene' (2.11), 'Talk about the story' (2.14), 'What's it all about?' (2.15), and 'Where and when?' (2.16).

2.1 Analysing trailers

Students watch a trailer (a short filmed advertisement) for a feature film. They then work in groups and use a worksheet to analyse and discuss the trailer.

LEVEL	**Intermediate and above**
TIME	**30–40 minutes**
MATERIALS	A trailer for a feature film; a worksheet for each student (intermediate or upper-intermediate) - see below.

PREPARATION   Cue the trailer. Make enough copies of the worksheet to give one to each student.

PROCEDURE

1 Draw two columns on the board. At the top of one of the columns, write the word *trailer*. Write the word *clip* at the top of the other. Explain to the class that a trailer is a short, filmed advertisement for a new film, and that a clip is a short piece from a film.

2 Ask the students to name any differences in content and style they would expect to find between a trailer for a film, and a two-minute clip from the same film. Write student answers in the appropriate column on the board.

EXAMPLE

Trailer	Clip
*The trailer will be **cut**.*	*The clip will be a complete sequence.*
The trailer may have graphics superimposed on it.	*There will be no graphics, unless they are part of the film.*
The trailer may have a voice-over commentary.	*There will be no voice-over commentary, unless it is part of the film.*

The idea of the trailer is to summarize the film in two minutes of viewing time, and to indicate what makes the film it is advertising uniquely different from other films on the cinema circuit.

3 Distribute the worksheet. Go through the questions on the worksheet to make sure students understand them.

4 Play the trailer 2–3 times. Pause for a few minutes after each viewing to give students time to make notes.

5 Put students into groups of two or three. Tell them to use the questions on the worksheet as a basis for discussion.

6 Conduct a feedback session with the students. Go through the questions and discuss the students' answers.

FOLLOW-UP   *Guidelines for making a trailer:* Students use the worksheet to compare the techniques used in several different trailers. Students then write a set of guidelines for making a trailer, for an audience that knows nothing about them.

REMARKS

In recent years, trailers have become more available on videotape and DVD. Many videos of popular films come with a selection of trailers at the beginning of the tape. Also, many DVDs and Collector's Edition videos of feature films include the original theatrical trailer (the trailer that was shown in cinemas) for the film. For a list of some videos and DVDs that contain trailers, see 5.3, 'Comparing trailers', on page 95.

Trailers are visually exciting and conveniently short, and can be used to great effect instead of film clips for many of the activities described in this book, for example, 2.6, 'Images and sounds', on page 41, 2.8, 'The memory game', on page 44, and 2.15, 'Where and when?', on page 57.

WORKSHEET   (intermediate)

ANALYSING TRAILERS
Discuss these questions in your group. Use the boxes to make notes about your answers.

What is the title of the film?	
When does the trailer give the name of the film? Why is this?	
What information about the actor does the trailer give? Why does it give this information?	
Which is faster, a trailer of a film or a clip from the same film? Why?	
What kind of music does the trailer use? What does the music suggest about the film?	
What information is at the end of the trailer? Why is this information at the end?	

Photocopiable © Oxford University Press

WORKSHEET   **(upper-intermediate and above)**

ANALYSING TRAILERS	
Discuss these questions in your group. Use the boxes to make notes about your answers.	
What is the title of the film that the trailer is advertising?	
Before what films at a cinema might this trailer be shown? Name some examples. For example: Think about whether the trailer is violent, sexy, or contains adult content or bad language. If it does, you wouldn't show this kind of trailer with, say, a Walt Disney cartoon for young children.	
At what point in the trailer do we find out the name of the film? Why is this?	
How is information about who is starring in the film presented? Why is it done in this way?	
How does the speed of the trailer compare to the speed of a clip from a film? Why is this?	
What kind of music is used on the trailer? What clues does this give us about the film?	
How would you describe the voice that delivers the voice-over? Why do you think this particular voice was used?	
What information is given in the very last **frame** of the trailer? Why do you think this information was placed at the end?	

2.2 Complete the timeline

**Students complete a timeline showing the sequence of
events in a film clip, and then produce a written summary
of the clip.**

LEVEL

Elementary to intermediate

TIME

30–40 minutes + time to write the summary

MATERIALS

A worksheet for each student (see below); a film clip that presents
a sequence of events with a beginning, a middle, and an end—any
straight narrative sequence will do, such as the one in *Notting Hill*
(1999) which begins with Anna Scott (played by Julia Roberts)
walking into Will Thatcher's (Hugh Grant) bookshop for the first
time and ends with her leaving the shop.

PREPARATION

Prepare enough copies of the worksheet to give one to each
student; cue the video to the beginning of the film clip.

PROCEDURE

1 Distribute the worksheet.

2 Tell the students they are going to see a film clip. Their task is
to watch and use the worksheet to make notes on the timeline
of each event they see in the clip.

3 Play the film clip in short sections, pausing at the end of each
major event to allow students to make notes on the worksheet.

4 Play the clip again, straight through without pauses. Students
watch the film and complete or change their notes if necessary.

5 Divide the class into small groups. Tell the groups to discuss
the film clip and compare their completed timelines.

6 Students use the notes in their timelines to write a one- or two-
page summary of all the events on the film clip.

VARIATION 1

Oral summaries: Instead of producing written summaries,
students can work in groups and take turns using their notes to
give oral summaries of the various events in the story to members
of their group. One student summarizes event 1, another student
summarizes event 2, and so on.

VARIATION 2

Order the events: If you are using DVD, you can use 3–4 selected
scenes from the DVD menu of a feature film, show the scenes out
of order, and ask the students to decide which scene comes first
in the film, which comes second, and so on. Ask students to give
reasons for their answers.

WORKSHEET

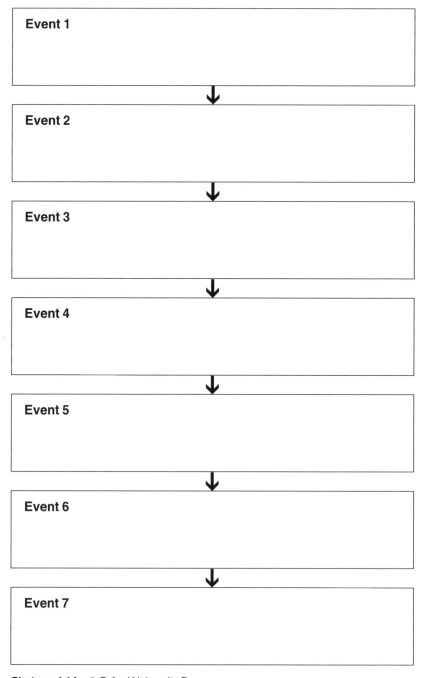

COMPLETE THE TIMELINE

Watch the film and complete the timeline. Use the boxes to take notes about each event that happens.

Event 1

↓

Event 2

↓

Event 3

↓

Event 4

↓

Event 5

↓

Event 6

↓

Event 7

2.3 Director's comments

Students think of *Why?* questions about a film clip, and then listen for the answers in a voice-over commentary on the film.

LEVEL	Advanced
TIME	**30–60 minutes**
MATERIALS	You will need a video or DVD that contains two versions of the same film. One is the normal version of the film with the complete soundtrack, the other consists of the normal version of the film with an additional soundtrack added, and on which you hear the director's and/or producer's **voice-over** commentary on how the film was made. There are some examples in *Remarks* at the end of this activity.
PREPARATION	Cue both clips to the beginning of the sequence.
PROCEDURE	1 Begin by playing the normal version of the scene, without the director's comments. The students discuss the **plot** and the characters. Ask them to describe the scene: where it is set, what it looks like, how the characters behave, and so on.
	2 Tell the students they will now have the opportunity to interview the director about the sequence. They must think of some *Why?* questions about the sequence.
	3 Elicit questions from the class and write them on the board.
	4 Now play the version of the scene with the voice-over commentary by the director and/or producer. The students listen for the answers to their questions.
	5 Elicit the answers from the students. Their questions may have been answered directly, by suggestion, or not at all.
	6 Play the commentary video again. This time pause the tape at points of interest and check that the students have understood.
	7 At the end of the activity, conduct a whole-class discussion centred on these questions:
	• *Why do you think the director shot the scene the way he or she did?*
	• *Do you agree with the way the director shot the scene?*
	• *Has doing this activity affected your appreciation of, or interest in, the film? How?*
FOLLOW-UP	As a homework assignment, students write a report on what the director, producer, or writer had to say about the scene. They might, for example, write their report in question and answer interview form.

REMARKS

'Collector's Sets' of videos of feature films often contain a version of the film which includes voice-over comments by the director on how or why particular scenes were shot the way they were, for example:

- the deluxe video collector's set of *The English Patient* includes a version on which director Anthony Minghella, producer Saul Zaentz, and author Michael Ondaatje provide a voice-over commentary on the shooting of the film;
- the collector's edition video of *The Usual Suspects* contains 'The Definitive Guide', in which the director and writer provide a voice-over analysis of the film;
- the DVD of *Notting Hill* contains a feature commentary with the director, producer, and writer.

2.4 Eyewitness

Students watch a film clip and then describe the events they have 'witnessed'.

LEVEL

Elementary and above

TIME

30–40 minutes

MATERIALS

A one- or two-minute film clip which shows an incident that a witness might be asked to describe or report on in real life, for example, for the police, family, or friends. Dramatic or unusual events with little or no dialogue work best, for example, an accident, a bank robbery, a fight, a mugging, or a pickpocketing incident.

PREPARATION

Cue the film.

PROCEDURE

1 Introduce the film clip by saying something like *Watch this*. Give no information about the content of the film clip, and do not tell the students that they will later be asked to act as witnesses.

2 Play the film clip straight through.

3 After students have watched the clip, ask the class a few general questions about what they saw, for example:

- *How many people did you see?*
- *What were they wearing?*
- *What happened first?*
- *What happened after that?*

Keep this questioning phase short and do not say whether particular answers offered by students are correct or incorrect. The purpose of the questioning is to give the students an idea of the kind of information they need to include in their description, and also to get them personally involved in the activity. Personal involvement in the activity tends to increase according to the amount that individuals disagree about the facts.

4 Divide the class into groups of three or four. Explain the task to the students. They should work together in their groups, preparing a reconstruction in note form of the event they witnessed in the film clip.

5 Volunteers take turns reporting their group's witness description of the event. As volunteers report, note the main points on the board.

6 Play the film clip again, with pauses and replays as needed to clarify particular points. Groups confirm or correct their own accounts of the event.

FOLLOW-UP

Each student writes a statement for the police, describing exactly what happened. In order to do this, you may want to replay the film clip, so that individual students can make their own sets of notes.

VARIATION

Split viewing: Divide the students into pairs. One student, the 'watcher', in each pair will watch the film clip, while the other student, the 'listener', sits with his/her back toward the screen and listens to the **soundtrack**. After the clip has been played, the listeners interview the watchers about what was shown on the screen. When students have completed the interviews to their satisfaction, play the clip again. The listeners confirm or correct their understanding of the events as described by the watchers.

Acknowledgement

This activity is adapted from Eddie Williams, *The 'Witness' Activity: Group Interaction through Video,* in Geddes, M. and G. Sturtridge (eds.), *Video in the Language Classroom* (London: Heinemann Educational Books, 1982), pages 69–73.

2.5 Hidden meanings

Students analyse and discuss the subtext of a scene.

LEVEL

Intermediate and above

TIME

20–30 minutes

MATERIALS

A short film clip of a conversation in which the characters clearly have strong feelings or reactions that they do not directly express in words, for example, a scene where a character's body language or facial expression conveys his or her attitude toward another character. Scenes with eight to ten utterances are usually long enough. The most useful scenes have some points of tension and contain no more than four speakers, all highly expressive actors.

PREPARATION   Cue the film clip.

PROCEDURE

1 Write the word ***subtext*** on the board. Depending on the level of the class, either elicit the meaning from the students or explain that we use the word subtext to refer to the hidden meanings in a conversation, expressed not by words, but other means such as intonation, tone of voice, timing, facial expression, gesture, eye contact, and posture.

2 Tell the class you are going to play a film clip in which the characters obviously have strong feelings about what is happening and what others are saying, but they do not express these feelings in words. Students should 'read between the lines' and find the *subtext,* by looking at the characters' bodies, watching their faces, listening to the tone of their voices, etc.

3 Play the film clip twice. The first time play it straight through with no pauses. The second time, use the **freeze-frame** control to pause the action at points where interpretive questions can be asked, for example:

- *What did the character say?*
- *Did the character mean what he/she said? How do you know?*
- *If not, what did he/she mean?*
- *What does character X think about what character Y said?*
- *What is Y thinking right now?*
- *How do you think X will respond to what Y said?*
- *How do you think this conversation will end?*

When dealing with the interpretation of hidden meanings, there may be no definite correct answers to some questions. Students can be encouraged to use expressions such as 'It's possible, but …', 'Maybe he/she's thinking …', or 'He/She might be wondering …'.

FOLLOW-UP 1   As follow-up work, students can do 2.11, 'Roleplaying great scenes', on page 49.

FOLLOW-UP 2   Tell students to imagine they are a character in the scene. They each write a letter from their character to a friend. In their letter they describe what happened in the scene and their thoughts about the events.

VARIATION   *Interior monologues:* Use a film clip in which one character says very little but obviously has strong feelings or reactions about what is going on. Ask students to imagine what the character is thinking and feeling, and to write an **interior monologue** (a passage of writing presenting a character's inner thoughts and emotions) from that character's point of view.

REMARKS

When using the freeze-frame control in step 3, it is not necessary to pause the film and ask questions after every utterance. The important thing is to ask the students to focus on the most important bits of hidden meaning and discover what is really happening between the people in the scene.

Acknowledgement

This activity is adapted from Barry Baddock, 'The subtext' in *Using films in the English Class* (Hemel Hempstead, Hertfordshire: Phoenix ELT, 1996), pages 31–6.

2.6 Images and sounds

Students watch a film clip and then call out any visual images and sounds from the film that immediately come to mind, along with their feelings or reactions to what they have seen. These student responses are then used as a springboard for whole class discussion.

LEVEL

Elementary and above

TIME

20–30 minutes

MATERIALS

A three- or four-minute clip of a key sequence in a film

PREPARATION

Cue the film clip.

PROCEDURE

1 Tell the students you are going to play a film clip. Their task is to watch and pay close attention to the images and the sounds.

2 Play the film clip.

3 After playing the clip, ask students to call out any visual images or sounds that immediately come to mind, as well as any feelings or reactions they have to the film. Write key words from their responses on the board. For example, students who have watched the scene in which violence erupts in *Do the Right Thing* (1989) might mention the images of the firemen and the water hoses and their personal reactions and feelings about the violence and racism displayed in the scene.

4 Conduct a whole-class discussion of the clip, centred on some or all of these questions:

- *What are some words you would use to describe the film?*
- *What, if anything, surprised you?*
- *What pleased you?*

- *What bothered you?*
- *What upset you?*

5 Proceed to more intensive study of the film clip for content and language. For a list of discussion questions that can be used with any film, see 4.1, 'Discussion topics', on page 77.

FOLLOW-UP

Allow 5–10 minutes for students to write their reactions to the film in their film journals. (See 7.3, 'Film journals', on page 132.)

VARIATION 1

Steps 3 and 4, the discussions phases of this activity, can be carried out in small groups.

VARIATION 2

In step 3, instead of asking students to call out the their responses, ask them to make a written list of images and sounds they recall. Students then get into pairs or small groups and compare lists.

REMARKS

This is an excellent activity for encouraging discussion of personal reactions to a film. In our experience, it is almost always better to allow for some small group or whole class discussion immediately after viewing, since that is when students will have the strongest reactions and best remember important details.

Acknowledgement

This activity is an adaptation of 'image-sound skimming' described by Richard A. Lacey in *Seeing with Feeling: Film in the classroom* (Philadelphia and London: W.B. Saunders Company, 1972).

2.7 Listen to the music

Students listen to the music used in the title sequence, and make predictions about the film.

LEVEL

Elementary and above

TIME

30–60 minutes

MATERIALS

Two films with typical atmospheric music over the titles (see the list of atmospheric music recommendations); a worksheet for each pair of students (see below).

PREPARATION

Cue each film at the opening of the title sequence. Make enough copies of the worksheet to give one to each pair of students.

WORKSHEET

LISTEN TO THE MUSIC		
Listen to the title sequences from two films, and fill in your predictions about each film.		
	Film 1	*Film 2*
Film genre		
Film title		
Time (historical period)		
Stars		
Opening scene		

Photocopiable © Oxford University Press

Atmospheric music recommendations

Film genre	*Example*
Thriller	*The French Connection* (1971)
Horror	*Jaws* (1975)
Romance	*Notting Hill* (1999)
Historical drama	*Anne of a Thousand Days* (1969)
Western	*Shane* (1953)
War film	*Lawrence of Arabia* (1962)
Adventure film	*Return to Snowy River* (1988)
Science fiction	*The Matrix* (1999)
Disaster film	*Volcano* (1997)
Comedy	*Dirty Rotten Scoundrels* (1988)

And a few interesting recommendations that might cause discussion:

Film genre	*Example*
Comedy, drama	*Danny, Champion of the World* (1989)
War	*Platoon* (1986)
Comedy	*Babe* (1995)

PROCEDURE

1 Preteach or revise key film genres, for example, *thriller*, *horror*, *romance*, *historical drama*, *western*, *war film*, *adventure film*, *science fiction (sci-fi)*, *disaster film*, and *comedy*. Elicit examples of each genre from the students, and write the titles on the board.

2 Divide the class into pairs and distribute the worksheet.

3 Tell the students they are going to hear the music from the title sequences of two different films. Their task is to work in pairs, discussing the music and filling in the worksheet with their predictions about the genre, title, time (historical period), stars, and opening scene of each film.

4 Cover the screen with a thick newspaper or coat and play the title sequence (sound only) of the first film.

5 Pairs discuss the music and fill in the worksheet with their predictions about the first film.

6 Repeat steps 3 and 4 with the second film.

7 Elicit the students' predictions and summarize them on the board.

8 Play the title sequences of both films with sound and vision, extending each into the opening scene.

9 The students compare their predictions with what they see and hear on the screen.

FOLLOW-UP

More advanced classes can describe the kind of music they would expect to hear in each genre.

2.8 The memory game

Students watch a film clip, and then talk about what they have seen and write down as many details as they can remember.

LEVEL

Elementary and above

TIME

10–15 minutes

MATERIALS

A 60–90 second film clip in which a wide variety of images are shown.

PREPARATION

Cue the film.

PROCEDURE

1 Divide the class into pairs.

2 Explain the task to the students. First, they are going to watch a short film clip. After viewing the clip, they should work with their partners, talking about what they have seen and writing

down as many visual details as they can remember. Depending on the level of the class, the students might mention concrete things such as objects or people, together with descriptions, processes, and actions, or more abstract things such as emotions or concepts.

3 Play the film clip.

4 Allow five minutes or so for pairs to discuss the film clip and make a list of all the details they can remember.

5 Pairs get together with another pair and compare lists. Who remembered the most?

6 Play the film clip again as a final check. Depending on the level of the students and the visual complexity of the film clip, you may want to pause at selected points and have student volunteers attempt to describe the details they notice on the screen.

REMARKS

In addition to being an enjoyable way to review and reinforce vocabulary, this activity is good for stimulating spoken language and discussion, and for encouraging students to pay closer attention to visual details than they might normally do. Focusing students' attention on visual details rather than spoken language has the dual effect of decreasing their anxiety about the language on the soundtrack and increasing their general understanding of the story as a whole.

At the same time, training students to pay closer attention to visual clues can help them to predict and understand specific items in the dialogue, especially in cases where there are links between the pictures and what the dialogue conveys, for example, you see Gene Kelly singing and dancing in the rain and in the song you hear 'I'm dancin' and singin' in the rain!' or you see a middle-aged woman, placing her hands on her hips and registering a surprised expression, look up at a very tall young young man and on the soundtrack you hear her saying, 'Oh my, you've grown tall!'

Paying closer attention to visual details such as gestures and facial expressions will also help students better to understand situations in which the speaker's body language does not necessarily back up what they are saying, for example, verbally they cooperate, but their gestures and facial expressions show dismay or alarm.

VARIATION

Team trivia quiz. Before playing the video, divide the class into two teams. Students watch the video and then each student writes down one or two questions about visual details in the film clip, for example, *What time did the alarm clock say? What password did the man type on the computer? How many books did Mary pick up?* Members of each team consolidate their questions into a list. Teams take turns asking members of the other team a question.

Individual members of each team take turns asking questions and responding. Score 1 point for each correct answer. If necessary, replay the film clip to check questions and answers. In any case, students should have a chance to view the entire sequence again at some point.

2.9 Point of view

Students watch a clip and describe the action from the point of view of one of the characters.

LEVEL **Intermediate and above**

TIME **20–30 minutes**

MATERIALS A film clip with a limited number of characters, all of whom have some part to play in the scene.

PREPARATION Check whether the clip is complete in itself or whether you need to provide a brief story **synopsis**; cue the film to the start of the chosen clip.

PROCEDURE 1 Explain the task to the students. They are going to watch a film clip and describe the action from the **point of view** of one of the characters on the screen. They need to observe and describe:

- what people do
- what they say
- their character's emotions about what he/she observes.

Students can give their description in the present or the past tense, but they should use the first person singular form (*I ...*) to express the character's personal attitude, emotions, etc.

2 Divide the class into small groups, one group per character. Or, alternatively, allocate the same character to all the groups so that you get a variety of opinions about one character.

3 Watch the clip with the students so that they get an idea of who their characters are. Make sure they understand the storyline. If necessary, give out the synopsis for the students to study.

4 Play the clip again. This time the students find words to describe their character's emotions and how the situation appears from the character's point of view.

5 In groups, the students make notes on and rehearse their point of view. Go round the class, giving help where necessary.

6 Each group nominates a 'speaker' who presents their character's point of view in the first person, for example, *I saw her come into the room, she was wearing ...* . Each group presents in turn.

7 At the end of the activity, the class discuss what they have learnt about the characters and the plot of the film.

FOLLOW-UP Students can write up their points of view for homework.

2.10 Predict the opening scene

Students use a video cover, magazine or newspaper advertisement, or poster to make predictions about what might happen in the opening scene of a film.

LEVEL **Intermediate and above**

TIME **30–40 minutes**

MATERIALS A film clip of an opening scene; the film's video cover, film poster, or illustrated newspaper or magazine advertisement; a copy of the worksheet for each group of 3–4 students (see below).

PREPARATION Cue the film clip; make enough copies of the worksheet to give one to each group of 3–4 students.

PROCEDURE

1 Remind the class that print materials such as newspaper and magazine advertisements, film posters, and video covers give us information about a film, and that we usually have expectations about what will happen in a film, based on what we have seen and read. Explain to the class that they are going to examine a video cover, magazine or newspaper advertisement, or poster (whichever you choose to use) and predict what might happen in the film.

2 Divide the class into groups of three or four.

3 Distribute one copy of the worksheet and one photocopy of the video cover, newspaper, or magazine advertisement to each group of students—or put the poster on a board or wall where all the students can have a good view of it.

4 Explain the task to the students. They should work together in their groups, examining the title, comments, picture(s), story outline, and any other information that may be included in the material. Then they should discuss what might happen in the story and what might happen in the opening scene of the film. Finally they should use the worksheet to summarize their ideas about what might happen in the opening scene.

5 Allow enough time for groups to examine the print material and complete the worksheet.

6 After groups have finished, ask for volunteers to summarize their group's predictions about the opening scene. Do not at this point say how accurate any group's predictions might be.

7 Play the opening scene of the film.

8 Conduct a whole-class discussion of the following questions:

- *Which group's predictions were closest to what happens in the opening scene of the film?*
- *How to do you feel about the opening scene? Is it interesting?*
- *How do you feel about the characters? Do you like them?*
- *Based on what you have seen and read about this film, would you be interested in seeing the whole film? Why or why not?*

VARIATION 1

As a follow-up or for homework, students can be asked to write a one- or two-page summary of, and/or their personal reaction to, the opening scene they have watched.

VARIATION 2

Students can discuss, as a whole class or in groups, what they think will happen in the next scene of the film:

- *Where and when will the next scene take place?*
- *Which characters will appear in the scene?*
- *What will happen?*
- *What are some lines of dialogue you will hear?*

After the discussion, play the second scene and ask students to compare their predictions with what actually happens in the scene.

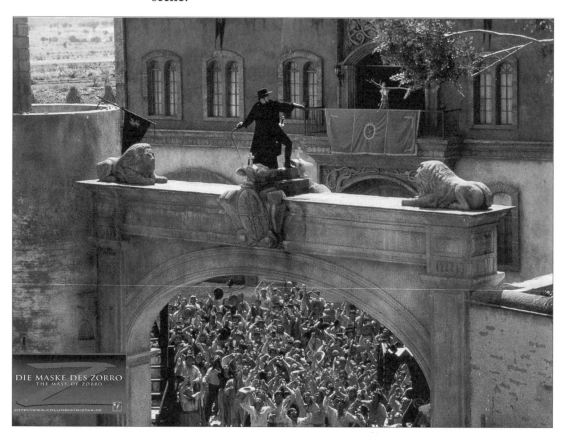

DIE MASKE DES ZORRO
THE MASK OF ZORRO

HTTP://WWW.COLUMBIATRISTAR.DE

WORSHEET

PREDICT THE OPENING SCENE	
Setting Where and when might the opening scene take place?	
Characters Which characters might appear in the opening scene?	
Key events What might happen in the opening scene?	
Dialogue What are some lines of dialogue you might hear?	
Other List any other details you think might be part of the opening scene.	

Photocopiable © Oxford University Press

2.11 Roleplaying great scenes

Students practise reading and performing famous scenes.

LEVEL

Elementary and above

TIME

20–30 minutes

MATERIALS

A clip of a famous scene from a film; a transcript of the scene for each student (see sample below).

PREPARATION

Cue the film; make enough photocopies of the transcript (see the sample transcripts) to give one to each student.

PROCEDURE

1 Divide the class into groups equal to the number of speaking parts in the scene and distribute the transcript. Tell the students they are all going to have the chance to be actors and play a part in a famous film scene.

2 Play the film version of the selected scene through a couple of times. Discuss any significant speech features used by the actors, for example, *What word does Annie stress most in 'There's a big spider in the bathroom.' What intonation does Alvy use in 'Hey, what is this?'*. Get students to practise those features using the transcript.

3 Students roleplay the dialogue as a sit-down reading task. Encourage students to use both *verbal* and *non-verbal* ways to express the thoughts and feelings of the characters.

4 Get volunteers to take turns performing the scene for the class.

FOLLOW-UP

As an extension of this activity, students working in pairs or small groups discuss the ways the scene might continue. Then they write up the imagined dialogue and roleplay it for the class.

VARIATION 1

Distribute the transcript and ask the students to practise reading the script *before* seeing the film version of the scene. Pairs or groups perform their interpretations of the scene for the class. Finally, play the film version of the scene to the students. Discuss the similarities and differences between the film and the students' interpretations.

REMARKS

1 This activity works best with scenes involving no more than 2–3 characters.

2 The kind of roleplay described in the basic version of this activity (sit-down reading) can be very useful with shy or reluctant students.

3 This activity is a good follow-up to 1.3, 'Famous film lines', on page 14.

4 For suggested sources of film scripts, see Appendix B, 'Internet resources for film', on page 146.

SAMPLE TRANSCRIPT

From *Annie Hall*

Annie, looking slightly distraught, goes to open the door to Alvy's knock.

ALVY   What's—It's me, open up.

ANNIE   *(Opening the door)* Oh.

ALVY   Are you okay? What's the matter? *(They look at each other, Annie sighing)* Are you all right? What—

ANNIE   There's a spider in the bathroom.

ALVY   *(Reacting)* What?

ANNIE   There's a big black spider in the bathroom.

ALVY   That's what you got me here for at three o'clock in the morning, 'cause there's a spider in the bathroom?

ANNIE   My God, I mean, you know how I am about insects—

ALVY   *(Interrupting, sighing)* Oooh.

ANNIE   I can't sleep with a live thing crawling around in the bathroom.

ALVY   Kill it! For Go—What's wrong with you? Don't you have a can of Raid in the house?

ANNIE   *(Shaking her head)* No.

         Alvy, disgusted, starts waving his hands and starts to move into the living room.

ALVY   *(Sighing)* I told you a thousand times you should always keep, uh, a lotta insect spray. You never know who's gonna crawl over.

ANNIE   *(Following him)* I know, I know, and a first-aid kit and a fire extinguisher.

ALVY   Jesus. All right, gimme a magazine. I—'cause I'm a little tired.

         (While Annie goes off to find him a magazine, Alvy, still talking, glances around the apartment. He notices a small book on a cabinet and picks it up.)

         You know, you, you joke with me, you make fun of me, but I'm prepared for anything. An emergency, a tidal wave, an earthquake. Hey, what is this? What? Did you go to a rock concert?

ANNIE   Yeah.

ALVY   Oh, yeah, really? How—how'd you like it? Was it—was it, I mean, did it … was it heavy? Did it achieve total heavy-ocity? Or was it, uh …

ANNIE   It was just great!

ALVY   *(Thumbing through the book)* Oh, humdinger. When—Well, I got a wonderful idea. Why don'tcha get the guy who took you to the rock concert, we'll call him and he can come over and kill the spider. You know, it's a—

         He tosses the book down on the cabinet.

This activity is adapted from "Teaching English With Great Movie Scenes", a presentation by Lisa Brickell and Jim Kahny at the 30th Annual International Summer Workshop for Teachers of English, Language Institute of Japan, Odawara, Japan in August of 1998.

More great scenes to use

The final scene of *Gone with the Wind*, where Rhett Butler walks out on his wife, Scarlett O'Hara.

The final showdown between Luke Skywalker and Darth Vader in *The Empire Strikes Back*, where they fight with light sabres.

The scene in *The Wizard of Oz* where the Good Witch Glinda arrives and tells Dorothy how to get back home to Kansas.

2.12 Show your emotions

Students identify and describe emotions displayed by characters in a film clip.

LEVEL	**Intermediate and above**
TIME	**30 minutes**
MATERIALS	A film clip of a very emotional sequence from a film; a worksheet for each student (see below).
PREPARATION	Choose a short film clip that shows a display of emotion; make enough copies of the worksheet to give one to each student.

PROCEDURE

1 Pre-teach vocabulary for describing different degrees and ways of expressing emotion, for example, *restrained, controlled, emotional, tight-lipped, lip quivering, mouth wide open, eyes neutral, eyes expressive, eyes staring, gesticulating, cold, cool, over the top, screaming, yelling, crying.*

2 Brainstorm with the class how different cultures express emotion in film, i.e. vocally, using body language, etc.

3 Tell the class you are going to show them a clip from an English-language film. They have to work out what is happening in the scene, and then identify and describe the emotions shown by the characters.

4 Play the clip once. Ask for volunteers to describe what happens in the clip, and to identify any emotions that they saw.

5 Distribute the worksheet. Tell the class they are going to see the clip again. This time they should concentrate on the emotions the actors show and take notes in the appropriate boxes on the worksheet. Ask them to try to include at least 2–3 different examples.

6 Play the clip again. Students work alone, completing their worksheets.

7 Ask the students to work in pairs and compare their answers.

8 Finish the activity with a whole-class discussion based on these questions:
   - *How did you feel about the emotion in the film? Was it just right, too little, or too much for the situation?*
   - *Does the scene work for you? If not, how would you change it?*

REMARKS

This activity works especially well with scenes from silent films, for example, the scene in *Blood and Sand* (1922) when the bullfighter (Rudolph Valentino) meets and falls under the spell of the Marquis's daughter, Doña Sol.

WORKSHEET

SHOW YOUR EMOTIONS			
Who? Which character displays the emotion?	**What?** What emotion does the character display?	**How?** How does the character display the emotion?	**When?** What is happening at the time the character displays the emotion?

2.13 Talk about the story

Students watch a film clip, then fill out a worksheet and discuss story elements such as plot, setting, and characters.

LEVEL

Intermediate and above

TIME

40–50 minutes

MATERIALS

A five- to ten-minute clip from a film that illustrates the literary elements of film: plot, **characters**, **setting**, point of view, mood, and **theme**, for example, the second sequence in *Citizen Kane:* a newsreel biography of the title character, Charles Foster Kane; a worksheet for each student (see below).

PREPARATION

Make enough copies of the worksheet to give one copy to each pair of students; cue the video to the start of the film clip.

PROCEDURE

1 Write the following terms on the board: ***plot***, *characters*, *setting*, ***point of view***, ***mood***, *theme*.

2 Explain to the class that the six words on the board are features that films have in common with works of literature such as novels or short stories. Go through the words one by one with the class to be sure students are familiar with their meanings. Definitions of these and other important film terms are included in Appendix A, 'Glossary of film terms', on page 141.

3 Divide the class into pairs and distribute one worksheet to each pair of students.

4 Explain the task to the students. They are going to view a film clip and then they are work together with their partners, discussing the clip and answering the questions on the worksheet.

5 Get the students to read through the questions on the worksheet, and make sure they understand them.

6 Play the film clip.

7 Students work with their partners, discussing the film clip and completing the worksheet.

8 Conduct a whole-class discussion based on the questions on the worksheet.

FOLLOW-UP

As a follow-up, ask students to think about their favourite films and choose one. Working individually, students use the questions on the worksheet to analyse their chosen film. Pairs or small groups of students then use their completed worksheets as a basis for discussion and comparison of their favourite films.

REMARKS

This activity works well when preceded by a discussion of the students' favourite films. (See 1.4, 'Favourite films', on page 17.)

WORKSHEET

TALK ABOUT THE STORY	
Plot (What are the main things that happen in the story?)	
Characters (What are their names?)	
Setting (Where does the story take place?)	
Point of view (Who is the narrator of the story?)	
Mood (What is the mood of the film?	
Theme (What is the theme of the film?)	

2.14 What's it all about?

Students create a script based on a freeze-frame picture from a film clip.

LEVEL **Elementary to intermediate**

TIME **50–60 minutes**

MATERIALS A one- or two-minute film clip of a very dramatic scene with two characters, each with something interesting to say in relatively easy-to-follow language.

PREPARATION Cue the film clip to a shot that shows the two characters interacting.

PROCEDURE

1 Write the following questions on the board:
   - *What's the situation?*
   - *Who are these people?*
   - *Where are they?*
   - *What are they doing?*
   - *What are they talking about?*

2 Divide the class into pairs. Tell the class they are going to see a **freeze-frame** picture from a scene in a film. They should study the picture and imagine all they can about the characters, the setting, and the situation. Ask students to think about the questions on the board as they look at the picture.

3 Display the selected freeze-frame picture on the screen for three to five minutes.

4 Students work in pairs, discussing possible situations or story-lines to go with the picture.

5 After pairs have discussed the picture for five or ten minutes, elicit some examples of situations and story-lines from student volunteers.

6 Students continue to work in pairs. Their task is to write a one- or two-minute script in which the freeze-frame picture they have studied has some part, and then practise performing their scenes with their partners.

7 Student pairs write their scripts and practise performing their scenes.

8 Pairs take turns performing their roleplays for the class.

9 Play the whole scene through. Students compare their scripts with the film clip.

2.15 Where and when?

Students watch a film clip, take notes about the pictures and words that give information about the setting, and then compare and discuss their notes.

LEVEL	**Elementary and above**
TIME	**20–30 minutes**
MATERIALS	A 3–5-minute film clip with a strong sense of setting in its narrative, for example, the scene near the beginning of *Notting Hill* (1999) where William (Hugh Grant) walks through a weekday market in the Notting Hill area of London and describes the neighbourhood in **voice-over**; enough copies of the worksheet (see below) for each student.
PREPARATION	Make copies of the worksheet for each student; cue the film clip.

PROCEDURE

1 Write the word *setting* on the board. Ask the class *What is the setting of a film?* As student volunteers give their answers, write key words from their responses on the board.

2 Explain to the class that the setting of a film (the time, place, and circumstances in which a film takes place) gives them a lot of information about the story, and that in this lesson they are going to look at the setting of a film.

3 Distribute the worksheet. Go over all the items on the worksheet to make sure the students understand the questions.

4 Explain the activity to the students. They are going to watch a clip from a film. As they watch, they should look for visual clues and listen for words that give information about the setting of the story. After viewing the clip, they should complete the worksheet.

5 Play the film clip.

6 Allow enough time for students to complete their worksheets.

7 When the students have completed their worksheets, divide the class into small groups and ask students to compare and discuss their answers.

8 Write the words *saw* and *heard* on the board. Conduct a whole-class discussion centred on the following questions:

- *What things did you see that gave information about the setting?*
- *What words did you hear that gave information about the setting?*

Write key words and phrases from the students' responses under the appropriate word, *saw* or *heard*, on the board.

VARIATION 1

Intermediate

In classes at intermediate level and above, students can discuss this additional question in step 8: *What aspects (costumes, music, etc.) gave the strongest sense of setting?*

VARIATION 2

Advanced

Advanced students can be asked to draw up a list of explicit and implicit techniques that **filmmakers** use to communicate information about setting to their audience.

WORKSHEET

WHERE AND WHEN?
1 When does the story take place, in the past, present, or future?
2 How do you know?
3 Does the film tell you the year, month, or season that the story takes place?
4 If yes, how does it do so?
5 What time of day does the scene take place?
6 How do you know?
7 Where does the scene take place?
8 How do you know?
9 Draw a picture of the setting and label the important things.

3 Creating film-related materials

In this chapter, students have the opportunity to try out their own filmmaking and directing skills in a series of activities related to planning, scripting, filming, sound, and editing. The activities expose students to the language of film and get them involved in the process of film creation through work in pairs and groups. None of these activities involve technical equipment, except for the video player, but they all allow students to experience and appreciate the excitement and challenges of the creative process.

Activities such as 'Design the remake' (3.2) and 'Writing film scripts' (3.9) encourage students to look at the process of creating a film. 'Storyboards' (3.8) invites students to imagine how they would visualize and present a piece of literary text on film. 'Establishing shots' (3.4) asks students to think about the all-important process of creating the mood and atmosphere of a film in the opening scenes. 'Create a new soundtrack' (3.1) and 'Sound dub' (3.7) encourage students to analyse the sound effects and dialogue in film and their effect on the audience, while 'Edit your own film' (3.3) looks at the editing process and asks students how many ways they can combine a sequence of images to create a particular effect.

Finally, two activities refer to the industry itself. 'In the news' (3.6) invites students to compare 'real life' stories with the **documentary** reality, and 'Film memorabilia' (3.5) considers the images of film stars as representatives of a country's cinema culture.

3.1 Create a new soundtrack

Students work in groups to create a script for an original voice-over soundtrack to go with the pictures on a film clip.

LEVEL	**Intermediate and above**
TIME	**40–50 minutes**
MATERIALS	A one- or two-minute film clip.
PREPARATION	Cue the film clip.

PROCEDURE

1 Divide the class into small groups and tell students they are going to watch a film clip without the sound. Ask them to imagine that the visual track (pictures only) belongs to another genre, such as a TV news report, a documentary film, or a TV advertisement. Their task is to work in groups and create a **script** for a voice-over to go with the pictures. Explain to the students that the goal is *not* to reconstruct the original film script. Instead, they should write a completely new and original text to go with the pictures.

2 Play the film clip with the sound *turned down*. The students in their groups watch the clip, discuss their ideas for a new soundtrack, and write a voice-over to go with it. You will need to replay the clip several times, until each group has completed a script to their satisfaction.

3 Ask groups to take turns performing their voice-overs for the class. Volunteers from each group read their script while you replay the film clip with the sound turned down.

4 Discuss the different scripts and the process of scriptwriting with the class. Use these questions:

- *Which script did you like best?*
- *Which one was most suitable for the pictures?*
- *What problems did you have when you were writing scripts?*
- *What problems did you encounter in performing them?*

FOLLOW-UP

Play the film clip with the sound *turned up*. Students compare their scripts with the original soundtrack.

3.2 Design the remake

Students outline a plan for a remake of a well-known film and then present their ideas to the class.

LEVEL

Lower-intermediate and above

TIME

45 minutes

MATERIALS

One worksheet for each group of students (see below).

PREPARATION

Make enough copies of the worksheet to give one to each group of 3–4 students.

PROCEDURE

1 Introduce the noun **remake** (a new version of an old film) to the class, and remind students that a lot of modern films are remakes of older films.

2 Elicit some examples of remakes from the class. If students have trouble thinking of examples, you may want to give a few examples of your own, for example, the many remakes of *The*

WORKSHEET

DESIGN THE REMAKE

1 Original title
What's the original title of the film?

2 Title of the remake
What title will you give the remake?

3 Genre
What genre will it be? Musical? Romantic comedy? Western? Detective? Horror film? Terrorist thriller? Some other genre?

4 Setting
Where and when will the story take place?

5 Cast
What actors would you cast in the main roles?

Main roles: *Actors who would play them:*

....

....

....

....

....

6 Theme music
What would you use for the theme music?

Adventures of Robin Hood (including the 1991 version starring Kevin Costner, and the 1973 Disney cartoon version) and *Romeo and Juliet* (including the 1996 version starring Leonardo DiCaprio and Claire Danes, and the 1961 musical *West Side Story*).

3 Divide the class into groups or 3–4 and distribute the worksheet.

4 Explain the task to the students. They should imagine they are film producers. Their job is to work together in their groups and write a plan for a remake of a well-known film. Groups should use the worksheet to summarize their ideas, which they will later present to the class. Encourage students to be as creative as they like. They might, for example, want to remake *Gone with the Wind* as a musical.

5 Groups work together, discussing their ideas and completing the worksheet.

6 Groups take turns describing their ideas for remakes to the class. The students vote on which idea they like best.

FOLLOW-UP 1   Students develop some scenes for their remake by working in small groups to create scripts for the characters in the proposed setting. (See 3.9, 'Writing film scripts', on page 75.)

FOLLOW-UP 2   Groups can create film posters or other advertisements for their remakes. (See 1.7, 'Film posters', on page 21.)

FOLLOW-UP 3   More advanced classes can work in groups and write a two- to three-page '**treatment**' for their proposed remake to show how they would 'treat' the story in a screenplay. Treatments can be written as a simple description or outline. They should generally use the present tense and give a full account of the story with all the characters, actions, and scenes, but without dialogue or individual shots.

3.3 Edit your own film

Students use a storyboard to present their ideas for editing a film sequence.

LEVEL   **Elementary and above**

TIME   **30–45 minutes**

MATERIALS   Copies of the camera movement worksheet and jumbled storyboard (see below).

PREPARATION   Make enough copies of the camera movement worksheet and jumbled storyboard to give one to each pair of students.

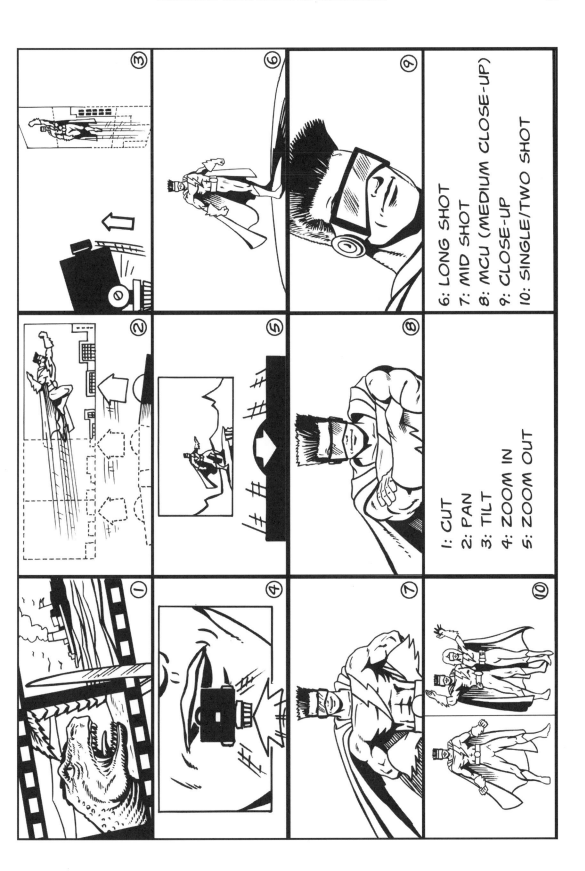

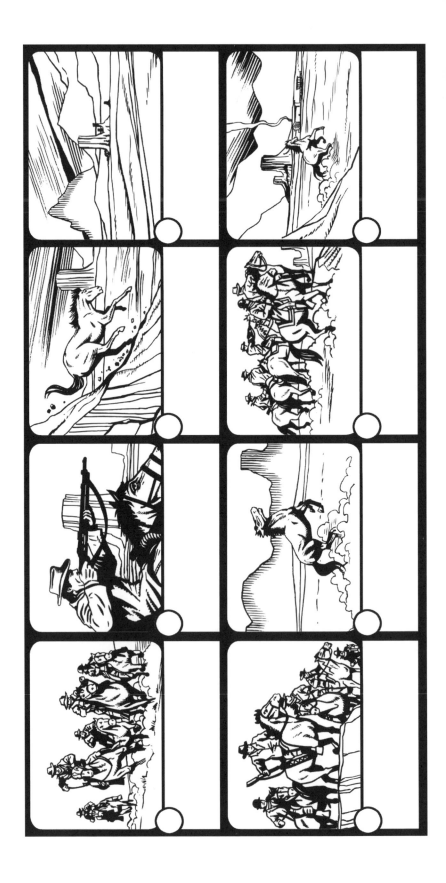

PROCEDURE

1 Divide the class into pairs and distribute one worksheet and one storyboard to each pair.

2 Go over the phrases on the worksheet with the class to make sure the students understand them. (See Appendix A, 'Glossary of film terms, on page 141.)

3 Go through the jumbled storyboard. Make sure the students understand the content of each storyboard picture.

4 Explain the task. Each pair will work together and decide how they want to **edit** the film **sequence**, using pictures from the jumbled storyboard. They may arrange the pictures in any order that makes sense to them, and they may alter any of the shots by using any one of the techniques in the camera movement chart.

5 Pairs complete the task by assigning a shot number to each picture on the storyboard, and by making a note next to the picture as to which camera movement they will use.

6 Pairs take turns presenting their storyboards and editing ideas to the class. Encourage listeners to ask the presenters to explain anything that is not clear.

7 At the end of the activity ask the class what they have learnt about the process and importance of editing.

3.4 Establishing shots

Students suggest establishing shots for the opening scenes of a number of films, and then compare their ideas with the establishing shots actually used by the directors.

LEVEL

Intermediate and above

TIME

40–60 minutes

MATERIALS

One worksheet for each pair or small group of students (see below); 3–4 films with different styles of opening, for example (see Appendix A, 'Glossary of film terms', on page 141):

> **title sequence** followed by **opening shots**
>
> opening shots before title sequence
>
> titles superimposed on opening shots
>
> **long shot**
>
> **close-up**

PREPARATION

Cue the films before the titles; make enough copies of the worksheet to give one to each pair or small group of students. Alternatively, you may wish to find films whose openings correspond to the conventions listed in the section above and write brief summaries, following the models in the worksheet.

PROCEDURE

1 Explain to the class that directors have different ways of setting or 'establishing' the mood for a film. These are called **establishing shots**. A director might:
   - begin with a long shot to show the location
   - begin with a close-up to give a sense of mystery
   - begin with the titles and let the music establish the atmosphere
   - have an opening scene and then introduce the title sequence
   - run the title sequence over the opening scenes so that the story is established before you see the director's name.

2 Divide the class into pairs or small groups and give each pair or group a copy of the worksheet.

3 Explain the task. Each pair or group should read the summaries on the worksheet and discuss the 'style' of the opening shots they would use to create the mood and atmosphere of the film.

4 Pairs or groups take turns reporting their ideas about the first film to the class.

5 Play the opening sequence of the first film.

6 Conduct a whole-class discussion centred on the following questions:
   - *Which group's/pair's conclusions were closest to the director's choice?*
   - *How effective was the director's choice?*
   - *Could the establishing have been done some other way? If so, how?*

7 Repeat steps 4–6 with each film clip.

FOLLOW-UP

As follow-up work to this activity, the students can do 2.10, 'Predict the opening scene', on page 47.

WORKSHEET

ESTABLISHING SHOTS

Film 1

A Man for all Seasons (1966)

This is a historical drama set in Elizabethan times. The director wishes to focus on the importance of the river as a means of transport and as a metaphor of passing time.

Film 2

Close Encounters of the Third Kind (1977)

This is a science fiction story. The director wants to begin the story with something that will shock and excite the viewers. He wants to suggest that we are in a strange new environment.

Film 3

The End of the Affair (1999)

This is a romance. The director wants to build up a sense of a person's life to establish the intimate mood of the story.

Film 4

Tomorrow Never Dies (1997)

This is an action film. The suspense needs to be established immediately and carried to a quick conclusion as a taster for the action to come.

3.5 Film memorabilia

Students examine and discuss memorabilia (items like stamps, postcards, and T-shirts) commemorating films or film stars, and then choose actors, films, or events to use on memorabilia, which celebrate or commemorate films in their home country.

LEVEL

Elementary and above

TIME

30–40 minutes

MATERIALS

Memorabilia such as postcards, stamps, clothes, cups, etc. on the theme of film.

PREPARATION

Gather enough memorabilia to give some items to each group of 3–4 students.

PROCEDURE

1 Divide the class into groups of three or four and distribute a selection of a few pieces of memorabilia to each group.

2 Explain the task to the students. Each group is to study the memorabilia they have been given and prepare a short presentation in which they present it to the class and explain what it reveals about:

- cinema in the country of origin
- the stars, films, or events shown
- the culture it comes from.

3 Students work together in their groups, preparing their group presentations.

4 Each group presents its memorabilia and its ideas to the class.

5 Conduct a whole-class discussion based on these questions:

- *What stars would you choose to commemorate or celebrate cinema?*
- *What films would you choose?*
- *What events in the history of cinema would you choose?*

As students respond, write the names of the suggested stars, films, and events on the board.

6 Get the class to vote from among the ideas on the board and choose the best five ideas.

FOLLOW-UP

Students can design their own memorabilia.

VARIATION

The whole-class work described in steps 5 and 6 above is suitable for monolingual classes. In multilingual classes, individual students (or groups of students) can each choose stars, films, and events from their own country, and then present their ideas to the class.

3.6 In the news

Students watch a film clip of an interesting event, and then write it up as a news story.

LEVEL

Intermediate and above

TIME

20–30 minutes

MATERIALS

A film clip which presents an event that could conceivably be reported in the news, for example, a robbery, murder, or earthquake, and which presents enough information to make use of the 'five Ws and an H' news-writing questions shown; a worksheet for each student (see below).

PREPARATION

Cue the film clip; make enough copies of the worksheet to give one to each student.

PROCEDURE

1 Introduce the activity by discussing news reporting with the class. Explain that the factual content of a news story usually answers questions based on the 'five Ws and an H' of an event:

- *Who* is it about?
- *What* happened?
- *When* did it happen?
- *Where* did it happen?
- *Why* and *how* did it happen?

If the 'five Ws and an H' technique is new to your students, you may want to use a newspaper article as an example to show the usefulness of the questions.

2 Distribute the worksheet. Go over the items to make sure the students understand what they should do.

3 Tell the students they are going to see a film clip showing an event that might be reported in a newspaper. Explain that you will play the film clip twice. Their task is to watch to get the general idea, and then to watch again and make notes to answer the questions on the worksheet.

4 Play the film clip twice. The first time the students watch. The second time, they watch and make brief notes to answer the questions on the worksheet.

5 When students have completed their worksheets, divide the class into small groups and get students to compare and discuss the items on the worksheet.

6 Finally, in the lesson or as homework, students work individually and write up a short news story based on the film clip.

IN THE NEWS
1 Who? Who is the story about? List the names of the important people in the story.
2 What? What happened? List the important events and facts of the story.
3 When? When did it happen? Be as specific as you can about the date and time.
4 Where? Where did the event take place?
5 Why and How? What reasons or causes were given for what happened?

3.7 Sound dub

Students translate a script from a film in their first language, and record it on audiocassette.

LEVEL

Advanced

TIME

45 minutes

MATERIALS

A short clip, about one minute long, from a film (original version) in the first language of the students; an audiocassette recorder with an extension microphone and a blank audiocassette.

PREPARATION

Prepare a transcript of the dialogue or commentary used in the extract, and make enough photocopies to give one to each student.

PROCEDURE

1 Divide the class into small groups and distribute the transcript. Explain that they are going to work together in their groups to prepare their translations. Remind them that they must give due consideration to:

- the language
- the speaking style and emotions of the speaker
- the translation of idioms and culturally specific expressions
- the lip movements of the actor who is speaking.

2 Students work in their groups, preparing their translations.

3 Groups take turns recording their translations on the audiocassette.

4 Play back the audio recordings together with the film, with the sound on the cassette player turned *up* and the sound on the video player turned *down*.

5 After playing each recording, members of the class give feedback on the translation.

6 After all the recordings have been played, ask for volunteers to say what they have learnt about the problems of translation and voice-over recording.

VARIATION 1

To make this activity more challenging, students can be asked to prepare their own transcripts of the dialogue or commentary on the film extract.

VARIATION 2

In multilingual classes, groups of students who have the same first language can work together to choose an extract from a film in their language, transcribe a minute or so of the dialogue, and then translate and record the dialogue into English. This can be done out of class as an assignment.

3.8 Storyboards

Students study a text, for example, a scene from a short story, novel, or play and create a storyboard.

LEVEL

Lower-intermediate and above

TIME

50–60 minutes

MATERIALS

A short scene from a short story, novel, or play; blank storyboards for each group; an example of a completed storyboard (see samples below).

PREPARATION

Make enough copies of the blank storyboard to give two or three to each group of 3–4 students, and enough copies of the text to give one to each group; either make an overhead transparency of the example of a completed storyboard, or make enough photocopies to give one to each group.

PROCEDURE

1 Divide the class into groups of three or four and give each group 2–3 blank storyboards and a copy of the text.

2 Display the example of a completed storyboard on the overhead projector, or give a photocopy to each group. Explain that filmmakers use storyboards to create picture outlines of scenes in a film. Each frame of the storyboard illustrates a key point in the drama, and the space under each frame space is used for writing a short description of the action, the dialogue, and other details such as camera angles, sound effects, and music.

3 Explain the task to the students. Tell them to work together in their groups, studying the text they have been given and deciding how they would present that text on film. They should break the text down into important points and decide the shots they would need to film the sequence, and then create a storyboard or picture outline of the scene.

4 Groups work together, discussing their ideas and completing their storyboards.

5 Groups take turns presenting their storyboards to the class and explaining the reasons for their choices.

FOLLOW-UP

In cases where a commercially-produced film of the text is available, teachers may play the film version for the class. Students can then compare and contrast their own ideas with those employed on the film. (See activity 5.1, 'Book to film', on page 89.)

SAMPLE TEXT

He gets up; goes to the telephone table in the hall, flipping through the telephone book. D. Pratt on Wisconsin. Carefully he notes it down. On the desk pad in front of him is another number, written months ago. 356–3340. Under it, in pencil: *Karen.* He looks at it for a long minute. Then, he gets up and goes again to the telephone.

The telephone is answered on the first ring. The voice is suspicious. "You want Karen? Who is this?"

"It's—I'm a friend of hers. From Northville."

"Northville." The voice goes flat. "Well, she isn't home right now. She's at school. Don't you go to school?"

Her mother, of course. Nobody else would take the trouble to cross-file him, or to be so damn worried. *No ma'am, no school. No time. Too busy being crazy.*

"Yes," he says. "I do. But we're off this week. Exams. Would you tell her I called? My name is Conrad—"

"I'll give her the message."

The receiver bangs loudly in his ear.

(Judith Guest: *Ordinary People*)

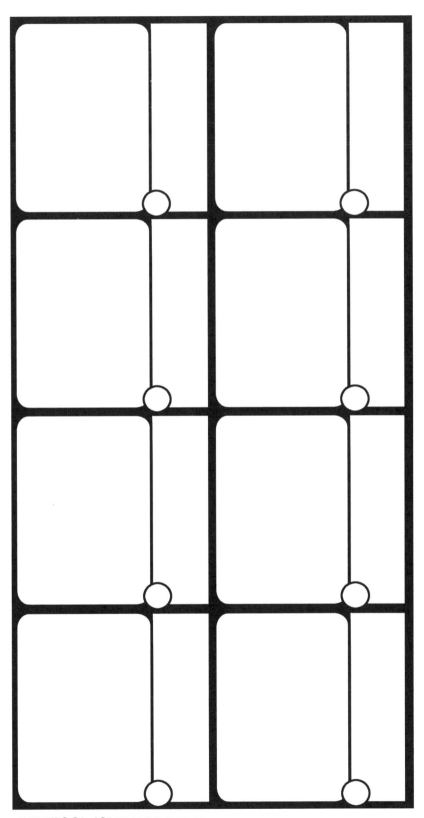

3.9 Writing film scripts

Students write a film script based on a text from a story or novel.

<table>
<tr><td>LEVEL</td><td>Intermediate and above</td></tr>
<tr><td>TIME</td><td>60 minutes</td></tr>
<tr><td>MATERIALS</td><td>Copies of the checklist (see worksheet below); a passage from a short story or novel.</td></tr>
<tr><td>PREPARATION</td><td>Choose a passage from a short story or novel that that you think would be suitable to be made into a film. Make enough copies of the checklist and the text to give copies to each group of 3–4 students. Alternatively, you may wish to get students to use a piece of writing from their textbook or class reader.</td></tr>
</table>

PROCEDURE

1 Divide the class into groups of three or four and distribute the checklist and text.

2 Tell the class to imagine they are **scriptwriters** who are writing a film adaptation of a story or novel. Their task is to work together in their groups and write a script based on the text they have been given.

3 Go over the checklist to be sure students understand what scripts usually look like. Tell the students that they should use the checklist to make sure their script is like a typical film script.

4 Students work in groups, discussing the text and writing their scripts.

5 When students are satisfied with their scripts, groups perform them for the rest of the class, perhaps with a few props, background music, or sound effects.

VARIATION 1

Students take an existing film script or play and create alternative versions of certain scenes. They might, for example, write a new beginning or a different ending, or add a new character.

VARIATION 2

Students create scripts for screen versions of popular fairy tales.

REMARKS

This activity works best when preceded by 1.1, 'Analysing film scripts', on page 10.

If time allows, this activity can be used together with 3.8, 'Storyboards', on page 71.

WORKSHEET

SCRIPTWRITING CHECKLIST

☐ Does each scene begin with a description of the setting?

☐ Is each scene numbered?

☐ Does each change of setting have a new scene number?

☐ Are the setting locations and times written in capital letters?

☐ Are the names of the characters written in capital letters (except where the names are part of the dialogue)?

☐ Are the names of the characters placed in the centre of the page?

☐ Is there a blank line between each character's speech?

☐ Are the stage directions enclosed in brackets?

☐ Are the stage directions written in the simple present tense?

Photocopiable © Oxford University Press

4 Responding to whole films

This chapter invites students to discuss films they have seen, sometimes with the help of individual sequences on video. However, the focus is on the complete film, rather than on the individual film clips, and students are encouraged to recall and compare the film sequences that have had most effect on them. The activities stimulate the use of spoken language in discussion by asking students to exchange ideas, compare points of view, and express opinions.

'Story frames' (4.3) and 'Story maps' (4.4) encourage and enable students at elementary and intermediate level to summarize plot lines, and to structure their thoughts and opinions about a film. 'Discussion topics' (4.1) and 'Favourite scenes' (4.2) encourage students to select the most vivid moments and scenes from a film and to compare their selections with those of other students. Finally, 'Writing film reviews' (4.5) helps students structure their ideas about a film and present them in written form.

Many activities in this chapter can be used in combination with activities found elsewhere in the book. Recommendations are given at the end of each lesson plan as appropriate, for example, 'Writing film reviews' (4.5) can be combined successfully with 'Comparing film reviews' (5.2).

4.1 Discussion topics

The students have a whole-class discussion based on their reactions to a film or film clip.

LEVEL

Intermediate and above

TIME

Variable

MATERIALS

No special materials are needed, but all the students need to have seen the same film or film clip.

PROCEDURE

Conduct a whole-class discussion based on any one or several of the following questions. Note that you do not need to ask *all* the questions. Select the one or ones that are most appropriate for the particular film or film clip, the level of the class, and the time available for discussion.

- *What did you like best about the film? Why?*
- *What, if anything, did you learn from the film?*
- *Was there anything you did not understand about the film? What was it?*
- *What were the filmmakers trying to tell us? Do you think they were successful? Why or why not?*
- *Which character in the film did you like best? Why?*
- *Which character did you like least? Why?*
- *Which events in the film were the most realistic?*
- *Which were the most unrealistic?*
- *Did you like the way music was used in the film? Why or why not? How would you have used music in this film?*
- *Did you like the way colour was used in the film? Why or why not? How would you have used colour in this film?*
- *Did the ending of the film seem appropriate? Why or why not?*
- *How would you have ended the film?*

FOLLOW-UP

Ask students to write a composition about any question they have discussed.

VARIATION 1

Small group discussion: Choose 2–3 questions that are appropriate for the film the students have watched and write them on the board. Ask students to discuss the questions in small groups. Follow this with a whole-class discussion. This variation is especially useful in large classes, or when some students feel shy about large group discussions. Such students usually appreciate having a chance to express their ideas in a small group.

VARIATION 2

Student-selected questions: Create a worksheet listing all the discussion questions above. Divide the class into groups and distribute the handout. Students in each group choose and discuss the questions of their choice. After fifteen minutes or so of discussion, volunteers give feedback.

VARIATION 3

Student-generated questions: Allow students five minutes to write down film-related questions they would like to discuss. Elicit the questions from the class and write them on the board. Conduct a discussion based on the questions suggested by the students.

REMARKS

Discussions of a film are most successful when they come straight after watching it. If students have a chance to see the clip immediately before the discussion, you might want to begin with 2.6, 'Images and sounds', on page 41 before going on to any of the questions above.

4.2 Favourite scenes

Students fill in a worksheet with information about three favourite scenes in a film they have seen and then report the information to the class.

LEVEL	**Intermediate and above**
TIME	**30–45 minutes**
MATERIALS	A worksheet for each group.
PREPARATION	Make enough copies of the worksheet (see below) to give one to each group of three students. All the students should have seen the same film.
PROCEDURE	1 Tell the class that they are going to discuss their favourite **scenes** in the film they have seen.

2 Elicit a list of memorable scenes from the class. If students have trouble getting started, help them, for example, 'I liked the scene where Bernice is in the barber shop,' or 'I thought the scene where Henry tries to get on the horse was very funny.' Write the suggested scenes on the board:

- *Bernice in the barber shop.*
- *Henry tries to get on the horse.*

3 Divide the class into groups of three.

4 Explain the task to the students. They should work in their groups and make a list of the scenes they liked in the film. Each person in the group should suggest one or two scenes.

5 Tell the students to number the scenes in the order preferred by the whole group.

6 Distribute the worksheet, and explain the task to the students. They should use the worksheet to write down information about the group's three favourite scenes: the setting, the characters, and what happens in each scene.

7 Each person in the group reports back to the whole class information about the setting, characters, and action of one of the group's three favourite scenes.

VARIATION With lower-level classes, instead of eliciting a list of memorable scenes from the class, as described in step 2, it may be more helpful if you present the students with a ready-made list of scenes from the film. You could write the list on the board, or distribute a copy of the list to each group.

WORKSHEET

FAVOURITE SCENES			
	scene 1	scene 2	scene 3
Setting (where the scene takes place)			
Characters (names of the most important characters in the scene)			
Action (the main things that happen in the scene)			

Photocopiable © Oxford University Press

4.3 Story frames

Students create a summary for a film they have seen by completing the sentences in a story frame.

LEVEL   **Elementary to intermediate**

TIME   **20–30 minutes**

MATERIALS   A story frame worksheet for each student (see below).

PREPARATION   Make enough copies of the story frame to give one to each student.

PROCEDURE

1 Write the following terms on the board: *setting, character, plot.*

2 Go over each of the terms with the class to be sure students are familiar with their meanings. Definitions of these and other important film terms are included in Appendix A, 'Glossary of film terms', on page 141.

3 Distribute the worksheet.

4 Explain the task to the students. They are going to use the worksheet to write about a film they have seen. They should fill in the name of the film they are writing about and then complete the sentences on the worksheet. With lower-level students, it may be helpful to go over 2–3 items on the worksheet and provide examples.

5 Students work individually, completing their worksheets.

6 Divide the class into groups of three or four. Students take turns reading their completed story frames aloud to their group.

FOLLOW-UP   As a follow-up activity, ask students to choose another film and fill out the frame again. Then, use the following questions as the basis of a whole-class discussion:

• *Are the settings similar or different? How?*
• *Are the characters similar or different? How?*
• *Are the plots similar or different? How?*

With discussion, students should begin to realize that although the setting, characters, and events may be different, the basic story structure is similar in different films.

REMARKS   Story frames provide lower-level students with a structure for organizing their ideas and generating responses to a film. They are also useful tools for developing an understanding of narrative structure and the elements of setting, character, and plot.

Depending on the ability of your students, you may want to simplify or add items to the frame.

WORKSHEET

STORY FRAME

Film title ....

Setting
The story takes place ....
....

I know this because I saw ....
....

I also know this because ....
....

Character
The main character in this film is ....
....

In the film, he/she ....
....

I think he/she is good/bad because ....
....

Plot
In this film, the problem begins when ....
....

Next, ...
....

Then, ...
....

Finally, the problem is solved when ....
....

4.4 Story maps

Students use a graphic organizer in the form of a 'story map' to sketch out the organizational structure of a film they have seen.

LEVEL	**Elementary and above**
TIME	**20–30 minutes**
MATERIALS	A blank story map worksheet for each student (see below).
PREPARATION	Make enough copies of the story map to give one to each student.
PROCEDURE	1 Distribute the story maps. If necessary, explain the terms in the six sections: *title*, *setting*, *characters*, **problem**, *events*, **solution**.
	2 Explain the task to the students. They choose a film they have seen and use the map to write information about it.
	3 Get students to read through the items and questions on the task sheet, and make sure they understand what they have to do.
	4 Students work individually, filling out their story maps.
	5 Divide the class into groups of three or four. Group members take turns reporting about the films they have described on their story maps.
FOLLOW-UP	In more advanced classes, story maps can serve as a lead-in to more creative and complex writing activities, such as 4.5, 'Writing film reviews', on page 84.
VARIATION	Distribute the story maps and go over the items on the form *before* students watch a whole film in the lesson, at a cinema, or on television as a homework assignment.
REMARKS	This activity works particularly well when preceded by 1.4, 'Favourite films', on page 17.
	Devices such as story maps and story frames help students find the basic elements of a story and provide a structure that helps lower-level learners generate responses in their own words. (See 4.3, 'Story frames', on page 80.) When overused, however, they may inhibit students' creativity. Once students have used these devices a few times, they are usually no longer needed.

STORY MAP	
Title of film	
Setting	*Characters*
Problem	
Events	
Solution to the problem	

Photocopiable © Oxford University Press

4.5 Writing film reviews

Students write a review of a film they have seen.

Intermediate and above

45–90 minutes, depending on the level of the class and whether reviews are written in the lesson or as homework.

A sample film review and a worksheet for each student (see below).

Make enough copies of the sample review and the worksheet to give copies of both to each student.

1 Ask the class how they decide which films they want to see, for example, friends' recommendations, newspaper or magazine advertisements, previews they have seen on television or in a cinema, or reviews they have read. After eliciting a few

answers, point out that some people use film reviews to decide whether they want to see a particular film.

2 Distribute the sample review and go over it with the students. Point out that a review is a piece of writing that gives basic facts about a film, a summary, and what the reviewer thinks about that film. The basic facts include the names of the main actors and the people responsible for making the film, for example, **director**, writer, or **cinematographer**. Elicit or show the students these in the sample review.

3 Use the sample review to provide examples of the following review-writing conventions:

- simple present tense used to describe and summarize the film
- actors' names enclosed in parentheses
- star-rating system used to evaluate film.

Talk about how the reviewer avoids revealing the ending or any information that might spoil the audience's surprise.

4 Tell the students they are each going to write a review of a film they have seen. Discuss with the class who the readers of their reviews might be. Could they, for example, publish their reviews in a school or class magazine, or on the Internet?

5 Distribute the worksheets and explain any new vocabulary items or concepts to the students.

6 Students work individually, completing the worksheet.

7 After students have completed their worksheets, ask them to work with a partner, comparing and discussing their answers to the questions on the worksheet.

8 In the lesson or as a homework assignment, students write their reviews.

VARIATION

To make the activity more challenging for upper-intermediate and advanced level students, omit steps 5–7 of the *Procedure* and ask students to write their reviews without using the worksheet.

REMARKS

Film reviews can vary from the very short and simple summaries that are printed in local newspapers and TV guides to the longer, critical reviews that are found in national newspapers and magazines, such as the example review of *The Sixth Sense*. A wide variety of film reviews are available on the Internet. For a list of Websites with links to film reviews, see Appendix B, 'Internet resources for film', on page 146.

This activity works particularly well when preceded by 5.2, 'Comparing film reviews', on page 93.

By Margaret A. McGurk
The Cincinnati Enquirer

On the surface, *The Sixth Sense* may seem like a supernatural thriller. But at its heart it is an intense, moving, thoughtful drama about the mysterious relationship between an exceptional little boy and a psychologist who wants to help him.

The child, Cole Sear (Haley Joel Osment), is literally haunted by a psychic gift. He can see the restless dead wandering near him, tormenting him with their fear and anger and confusion.

It is too much to bear for a little boy; he knows that, but he doesn't know what do to about it. He can't even confide in his loving single mother (Toni Collette), who is wracked with worry over him.

Psychologist Malcolm Crowe (Bruce Willis), is haunted, too, by his failure to rescue Vincent (Donnie Wahlberg), a patient he once treated. Cole seems to offer Malcolm a chance to redeem himself, even if the case seems to put even more distance between the psychologist and his wife (Olivia Williams).

Fair warning: The resolution of this story depends on a surprise revealed near the end of the film. The revelation casts a new light on the entire story, and makes sense of certain details that at first seemed peculiar, if not downright wrong.

Young Haley Joel Osment—who was nominated for an Emmy for his role as a dying boy on *Ally McBeal*—puts on a stunning display of depth and sensitivity as the precocious, articulate but profoundly sad child. Mr. Willis is astonishingly right in this role. "Subtle" is not a word I have often used in connection with his work, but in *The Sixth Sense* he is subtlety itself, a model of restraint and empathy.

The Sixth Sense is a quiet film, punctuated by a smattering of heart-stopping shocks. In fact, its stillness is unsettling, like the slashes of red that interrupt the muted grays and browns that shroud the action.

Cinematographer Tak Fujimoto captures the eerie scene with clarity and purpose, without resorting to corny horror-film clichés, and composer James Newton Howard contributes an evocative, understated score.

Writer-director M. Night Shyamalan's earlier film *Wide Awake* also focused on a little boy working out the connection between this world and the next.

Here he has crafted a story that is far more complex than it seems at first glance, a meditation on the paradoxical gap between the living and the dead, the invisible world that is at once vast and intimate.

It is no small accomplishment to find a new way to tell a ghost story. Mr. Shyamalan and company have done it by aiming straight for the heart. The result is a film that hits home in a way you won't soon forget.

WORSHEET

FILM REVIEW

1 What is the title of the film? ....

2 Who are the main actors in the film and what roles do they play?

....

....

3 Who directed the film?...

4 Who wrote the screenplay?..

5 Is this film like any other film you have seen? If so, what film is it like?

....

6 Who are the main characters in the story?...

....

7 What is the setting?...

8 What is the film about? Summarize the story (without the ending!) in no more than five
   sentences. Remember that your readers want to know enough about the film to make a
   decision about going to see it, but not so much that there's no need to go.

....

....

....

....

9 What is your opinion of the actors and the acting?

....

....

10 Do you recommend this film? If so, what sort of people will enjoy seeing it?

....

....

11 What star rating do you give this film? (☆☆☆☆ = excellent, ☆☆☆ = better than most,
    ☆☆ = average, ☆ = below average, no stars = poor)

....

5 Making comparisons

In this chapter, students compare different elements of film, different versions of films, or film-related materials.

'Book to film' (5.1) allows students to compare a film version of a novel with the original novel. 'Drama vs. documentary' (5.12) allows students to do the same, but this time the comparison is with a real-life activity. 'Culture check' (5.4), a similar kind of activity, invites students to analyse and discuss the image of their culture, as portrayed in foreign films.

Many successful films are remade, and the changes in plot, characters, and setting make interesting material for comparison. 'Original vs. remake' (5.10) explores this by getting students to analyse and discuss similarities and differences between scenes in different versions of a film. 'Comparing film reviews' (5.2) and 'Comparing trailers' (5.3) encourage students to analyse and compare different approaches to publicity and the very different reactions of critics to films they have reviewed.

A number of activities in this chapter focus on technical issues of translation, subtitling, and **dubbing**, and the effects these processes have on the audience. 'Film translation' (5.6) and 'From subtitles to pictures' (5.7) explore the effects of subtitles and translation on what is said in a film when it plays to a different national audience from its original version. 'What's the title?' (5.11) explores how titles of films change across languages, while 'How have they changed?' (5.9) examines how the choice of an actor to dub a role affects how a well-known actor is perceived in a foreign culture. How does Sean Connery appear when speaking Chinese, for example?

Finally, in looking at national cinema styles and production values, 'Hollywood style vs. national style' (5.8) invites students to compare national styles and values with those of the Hollywood imported films that tend to dominate our screens.

5.1 Book to film

Students compare an extract from a novel, short story, or graded reader with the film version of the same scene.

LEVEL	**Lower-intermediate and above**
TIME	**45–90 minutes, depending on the scene you choose.**
MATERIALS	An extract from a novel, short story, or graded reader, which has been made into a film and is available on video (see sample below); the same extract in a clip from the film version; copies of the worksheet (see below).
PREPARATION	Cue the film; make enough copies of the worksheet to give one to each pair of students.
PROCEDURE	

1 Tell the class you are going to read an extract from a novel (or short story or reader) that has been made into a film. Tell them they should listen carefully and picture the scene in their minds.

2 Read the extract to the class. Make your reading as expressive and interesting as possible.

3 Ask the students to work alone and write a paragraph that describes the main characters, the setting, and what happened in the story, in their own words.

4 Ask the students to work in pairs, comparing the paragraphs they have written.

5 Distribute the worksheet.

6 Tell the class that they are going to watch a film version of the scene they have summarized. Ask them to close their eyes again and picture the setting and each of the characters. Allow the students a minute or so to do this.

7 Tell the students to watch the video and think about the similarities and differences between the film and the book. Play the film version of the scene.

8 Ask the students to work in pairs, completing the worksheet with information about the book and film versions of the scene. Play the film again if necessary.

9 Follow up with a whole-class discussion based on these questions:

- *Did the setting look the way you had imagined it?*
- *Did the characters look the way you thought they would?*
- *Was the storyline the same as in the book?*
- *If anything was different, why do you think the producer changed it?*

- *Which did you like better, the book or the film version of the scene? Why?*
- *Do you think you would feel differently if you had seen the film first and then listened to (or read) the book? Why or why not?*

VARIATION 1

Instead of reading the extract to the students, distribute printed copies of the text for students to read alone or in groups.

VARIATION 2

Instead of using an extract from a novel or short story, use a scene from a play that has been adapted to the screen.

**VARIATION 3
(for lower levels)**

By simplifying the reading passage (or using a graded reader version of a film title) and/or by doing the oral reading twice the level can effectively be lowered.

SAMPLE TEXT

After much thought, I came up with a brilliant plan. I concocted a way for Rich to meet my mother and win her over. In fact, I arranged it so my mother would want to cook a meal especially for him ... .

The night of the dinner I sat in the kitchen watching her cook, waiting for the right moment to tell her about our marriage plans, that we had decided to get married next July, about seven months away. She was chopping eggplant into wedges, chattering at the same time about Auntie Suyuan: "She can only cook looking at a recipe. My instructions are in my fingers. I know what secret ingredients to put in just by using my nose!" And she was slicing with such ferocity, seemingly inattentive to her sharp cleaver, that I was afraid her fingertips would become one of the ingredients of the red-cooked eggplant and shredded pork dish.

I was hoping she would say something first about Rich. I had seen her expression when she opened the door, her forced smile as she scrutinized him from head to toe, checking her appraisal of him against that already given to her by Auntie Suyuan. I tried to anticipate what criticisms she would have.

Rich was not only <u>not</u> Chinese, he was a few years younger than I was. And unfortunately, he looked much younger with his curly red hair, smooth pale skin, and the splash of orange freckles across his nose. He was a bit on the short side, compactly built. In his dark business suits, he looked nice but easily forgettable, like somebody's nephew at a funeral. Which was why I didn't notice him the first year we worked together at the firm. But my mother noticed everything.

"So what do you think of Rich?" I finally asked, holding my breath.

She tossed the eggplant in the hot oil and it made a loud, angry hissing sound. "So many spots on his face," she said.

I could feel the pinpricks on my back. "They're freckles. Freckles are good luck, you know," I said a bit too heatedly in trying to raise my voice above the din of the kitchen.

"Oh?" she said innocently.

"Yes, the more spots the better. Everybody knows that."

She considered this a moment and then smiled and spoke in Chinese: "Maybe this is true. When you were young, you got the chicken pox. So many spots, you had to stay home for ten days. So lucky, you thought."

WORKSHEET

BOOK TO FILM		
	Book	**Film**
Setting Where and when does the story take place?		
Characters What are the names of the main characters? Describe their physical appearance and personality.		
Events What happens in the scene?		
Other Did you notice any other similarities or differences between the book and film?		

I couldn't save Rich in the kitchen. And I couldn't save him later at the dinner table.

He had brought a bottle of French wine, something he did not know my parents could not appreciate. My parents did not even own wine glasses. And then he also made the mistake of drinking not one but two frosted glasses full, while everybody else had a half-inch "just for taste."

When I offered Rich a fork, he insisted on using the slippery ivory chopsticks. He held them splayed like the knock-kneed legs of an ostrich while picking up a large chunk of sauce-coated eggplant. Halfway between his plate and his open mouth, the chunk fell on his crisp white shirt and then slid into his crotch. It took several minutes to get Shoshana to stop shrieking with laughter.

And then he had helped himself to big portions of the shrimp and snow peas, not realizing he should have taken only a polite spoonful, until everybody had had a morsel.

He had declined the sautéed new greens, the tender and expensive leaves of bean plants plucked before the sprouts turn into beans. And Shoshana refused to eat them also, pointing to Rich: "He didn't eat them! He didn't eat them!"

He thought he was being polite by refusing seconds, when he should have followed my father's example, who made a big show of taking small portions of seconds, thirds, and even fourths, always saying he could not resist another bit of something or other, and then groaning that he was so full he thought he would burst.

But the worst was when Rich criticized my mother's cooking, and he didn't even know what he had done. As is the Chinese cook's custom, my mother always made disparaging remarks about her own cooking. That night she chose to direct it toward her famous steamed pork and preserved vegetable dish, which she always served with special price.

"Ai! This dish not salty enough, no flavour," she complained, after tasting a small bite. "It is too bad to eat."

This was our family's cue to eat some and proclaim it the best she had ever made. But before we could do so, Rich said, "You know, all it needs is a little soy sauce." And he proceeded to pour a riverful of the salty black stuff on the platter, right before my mother's horrified eyes.

And even though I was hoping throughout the dinner that my mother would somehow see Rich's kindness, his sense of humour and boyish charm, I knew he had failed miserably in her eyes.

Amy Tan: *The Joy Luck Club*

ANOTHER SCENE TO ANALYSE

Students can compare a scene from *The English Patient* (1996) where the army sapper takes the nurse to see the frescoes in an old church.

Acknowledgement

This activity is based on Donna Lloyd-Kolkin and Kathleen R. Tyner "Print vs. Electronic" in *Media and You* (Englewood Cliffs, NJ: Educational Technology Publications, 1991), pages 97–8.

5.2 Comparing film reviews

Students work in pairs to compare and discuss two different reviews of the same film.

LEVEL	**Intermediate and above**
TIME	**50–60 minutes**
MATERIALS	A worksheet for each student (see below); two published reviews of the same film.
PREPARATION	Label the reviews 'A' and 'B' and make enough copies to give one set to each pair of students. Make enough copies of the worksheet to give one to each student.

PROCEDURE

1 Ask the class to predict the kind of information they would expect to find in a film review. Student responses are likely to include items such as the following:

- title of the film
- name of the reviewer
- names of the actors and the roles they play
- name of the director
- reviewer's opinion of the film.

  As student volunteers mention their ideas, write key words from their responses on the board.

2 Distribute the worksheet and tell the students they are going to use it to compare two different reviews of the same film. Go over all the questions to make sure students understand.

3 Divide the class into pairs, and give one set of both reviews to each pair.

4 Explain the task to the students. Each student will read one of the reviews and answer the questions about the review in the appropriate column of the worksheet. When both students have completed their notes, pairs should use the worksheets to compare the information they have gathered from the reviews and fill in the remaining column on their worksheets.

5 When students have finished, conduct a whole-class discussion centred on this question: *Based on the reviews you have read and talked about, would you like to see the film? Why or why not?*

FOLLOW-UP

Ask students to write their own reviews of films they have seen. (See 4.5, 'Writing film reviews', on page 84.)

VARIATION

Students who have access to the Internet can use any of several websites to locate and compare two reviews of a film of their own choice. (See Appendix B, 'Internet resources for film', on page 146.)

WORSHEET

COMPARING FILM REVIEWS		
	Review A	**Review B**
What's the title of the review?		
Where did the review appear? If it is an Internet reference, give that.		
What's the name of the reviewer?		
Does a photo accompany the review? If so, who or what is shown in the photo?		
What features of the film does the reviewer discuss?		
What features of the film, if any, does the reviewer like?		
What features of the film, if any, does the reviewer dislike?		
Does the reviewer recommend seeing the film?		
What star rating, if any, does the reviewer give the film?		
Write one or two sentences summarizing the reviewer's opinion of the film.		

5.3 Comparing trailers

Students watch trailers for three different films, take notes, and discuss which trailer they think is the best.

LEVEL

Intermediate and above

TIME

30–40 minutes

MATERIALS

Videos of three different **trailers**. Many videos of films have trailers of other films available from the distributor, and DVDs of films often include the original **theatrical trailer** for the featured film (see list).

PREPARATION

Cue the tapes or DVDs to the beginning of the trailers.

PROCEDURE

1 Write the word *trailer* on the board. Elicit the meaning of the word, as it relates to cinema, from the class. If students don't know, explain that a trailer is a short, filmed advertisement for a film. Tell them that trailers are often shown in cinemas before the main film, and that sometimes trailers are shown on television to advertise recent films.

2 Explain the task to the class. Students should work in pairs or groups of three or four. They will watch three film trailers. They should note:

- the title
- the star
- the film genre
- why the producers think you should see each film.

3 Play each trailer twice (or more if necessary). Allow enough time after each viewing for the groups to talk about the trailer, and make notes.

4 Elicit answers from the class and conduct a whole-class discussion based on these questions:

- *In your opinion, which was the best trailer? Why?*
- *Which film would you prefer to see? Why?*

5 At the end of the session, the class vote on the best trailer and which film they would prefer to watch.

FOLLOW-UP

In their groups, or as a whole-class activity, students can discuss how each trailer could be improved.

Some DVDs that contain trailers:

Amadeus (1984),
Warner Studios
Emma (1996),
Miramax Films

Being John Malkovich (1999),
Universal Pictures
Casablanca (1943),
Warner Home Video

Chariots of Fire (1981),
Warner Studios
Four Weddings and a Funeral
(1994), MGM
Gone with the Wind (1939),
Warner Home Video
Henry V (1989), MGM
Notting Hill (1999),
Universal Studios
Shakespeare in Love (1998),
Miramax Films

The Sixth Sense (1999),
Buena Vista Pictures
Titanic (1997),
Paramount
To Kill a Mockingbird (1962),
Universal Studios
The Wings of the Dove (1997),
Miramax Films
Young Frankenstein (1974),
20th Century Fox

5.4 Culture check

Students analyse and discuss the view of their culture in a film made in Britain or the US.

LEVEL

Intermediate and above

TIME

30–45 minutes

MATERIALS

A clip from a US or British film showing a scene based in the students' own culture

PREPARATION

Cue the film clip.

PROCEDURE

1 Write the words *stereotypical*, *idealized*, and *old-fashioned* on the board. Elicit or, if necessary, explain the meanings of the words:

  • *stereotypical:* oversimplified or over generalized
  • *idealized:* existing only in the mind or imagination
  • *old-fashioned:* out of date.

2 Tell the students they are going to view a film clip in which the action takes place in their own culture. Explain that you will play the clip twice. The first time, they will simply watch. The second time, they should watch and note down anything that they feel is stereotypical, idealized, or old-fashioned.

3 Play the film clip twice. The first time the students simply watch. The second time, they watch and make their notes.

4 Divide the class into groups of three or four. Explain the task to the students. They should work in their groups, comparing and discussing their notes, and compiling a written list of all the things in the film they think misrepresented their culture. If they liked the presentation of their culture they can say why they thought it was accurate.

5 Groups work together, comparing their notes and creating their lists.

6 Get student volunteers from each group to report their group's ideas to the class.

7 Conduct a whole-class discussion centred on this question: *How do you feel about the way your culture is portrayed in this clip? Why?*

VARIATION

This activity works well with monolingual classes. However, in multilingual classes, it can be carried out as project work. Individual students or groups of students show film clips to the class, point out the cultural errors, and then respond to questions and comments from the class.

5.5 Cuts

Students watch two film clips, describe what they see, and note the shots used.

LEVEL

Intermediate and above

TIME

50 minutes

MATERIALS

Two film clips. One clip must have long continuous camera shots with no cuts. The long, single **tracking shots** used in the opening scenes of Robert Altman's *The Player* (1992) and Orson Welles' *Touch of Evil* (1958) are two well-known examples. The other clip should rely on quick cutting to get its effects. Steven Spielberg's *Raiders of the Lost Ark* (1981) has many examples. Copies of film clip worksheet (see below).

PREPARATION

Cue the film clips; make enough copies of the worksheet to give one to each student.

PROCEDURE

1 Distribute the worksheet, and explain the task to the students. They are going to watch two film clips. They should note down what they see in the 'Description' column for each clip.

2 Play each clip. Students make notes about each clip. If necessary, play the clips a second time.

3 Students work in pairs, comparing their notes.

4 Elicit the descriptions from the class.

5 Write the words *shot* and *editing* on the board. Depending on the level of the class, explain the meanings of the terms to the students, or elicit the meanings from the students:

- *shot:* a unit of film in which the camera does not stop running
- *editing:* the process of putting a film together from its various shots and soundtracks to achieve a particular effect.

WORKSHEET

Film Clip 1		Film Clip 2	
Description	Shots	Description	Shots

6 Tell the class they are going to watch the clips again. This time they should divide what they see into shots. To help students, tell them to ask themselves this question: *When did the camera stop and then start again?* Explain that each time the camera starts again, a new shot begins.

7 The class watch, and for each clip they fill in the second column of the worksheet with the numbers of the different shots. If necessary, play the clips more than once.

8 Elicit the information from the class. Then play the clips one more time. The students identify the shots.

9 If you wish, the class can discuss the effect of the editing on each clip.

FOLLOW-UP

As a follow-up activity, advanced classes can write about or debate the following subject: 'Editing, not cinema, is the art of the twentieth century.'

5.6 Film translation

Students compare the original dialogue of a film clip with that shown in the subtitles (or heard on a dubbed version) in their first language. This activity is only suitable for monolingual classes.

LEVEL

Intermediate and above

TIME

30–40 minutes

MATERIALS

A clip of a film sequence which has been subtitled or dubbed into the students' first language, and which shows differences between the original language and first language versions of the dialogue; a script of the original English-language dialogue of the sequence. (See Appendix B, 'Internet resources for film', page 146, for links to script sources.)

PREPARATION

Make enough copies of the script to give one to each student.

PROCEDURE

1 Distribute the script and go over it with the students. Make sure they understand:
   • the situation
   • the plot
   • important language and idioms.

2 Tell the students that you are going to play a film clip. They should watch and decide what differences there are between the script they have studied and what they see or hear on the screen. Don't give any further information about what the

students will see and hear, in order to give them maximum opportunity for observation and discussion.

3 Play the film clip.

4 Ask the students if they noticed any differences between the screen version and the script. Elicit the differences.

5 Tell the class that they are going to watch the film clip again. This time they should follow along with their script and mark down any differences they notice.

6 Play the film clip again, more than once if necessary. This time the students follow the script and note any differences.

7 Elicit differences from the class.

8 Start a class discussion about why the changes took place. Explain the limitations of subtitling (or dubbing):

- subtitling—limited by the number of words that can go into a line
- dubbing—limited by the demands of **lip-synching**. (See Appendix A, 'Glossary of Film Terms', on page 141.)

Ask the students if there are other differences they notice, for example, changes in idioms or the use of 'bad' language.

VARIATION 1

For more advanced classes, you could discuss the effects of these kinds of problems on dubbing and subtitling:
- censorship *(bad language)*
- language *(a phrase must be translated differently)*
- different idioms
- cultural appropriacy *(concepts needing more or less explanation)*
- time and pace *(things taking longer to say)*
- lip synchronization *(the need to make the actor's lip movements correspond)*.

VARIATION 2

Multilingual classes could work on films into or out of their own language, and report back to the class on interesting differences.

FOLLOW-UP

The students could do this activity with films they watch at home, particularly if the films are subtitled. They could note down and report to the class examples of any changes they notice.

REMARKS

Films in DVD format are often good for this activity because many contain the original version of the film together with a dubbed version and a subtitled version.

5.7 From subtitles to pictures

Students watch the subtitles of a clip with no pictures or sound, then subtitles and sound with no picture, and finally the pictures and sound and subtitles, and discuss a series of questions about the clip. The activity as described here is only suitable for monolingual classes. However, the variation described below, *From captions to pictures*, is suitable for multilingual classes.

LEVEL

Elementary and above

TIME

20–30 minutes

MATERIALS

A two- or three-minute film clip with subtitles in the students' first language.

PREPARATION

Prepare a list of 5–6 questions about the scene in the film clip, for example:

- *Where does the scene take place?*
- *How many people are in the scene?*
- *How old are they?*
- *What are they wearing?*
- *What is their relationship?*
- *What are they doing?*

Cue the film clip and cover the screen so that only the subtitles are visible.

PROCEDURE

1 Write the list of questions on the board.

2 Tell the students that they are going to see the subtitles of a scene *without seeing the pictures.* Their task is to read the subtitles and predict what they will see in the pictures.

3 Play the film clip *without sound.*

4 Tell the students to work in groups of three or four, discussing the questions and giving reasons for their answers.

5 Play the film clip again, this time *with sound.*

6 Groups discuss the questions again, taking into consideration the voices, sound effects, and so on, that they have heard on the soundtrack.

7 Play the clip a third time, this time *with sound and pictures.*

8 Groups discuss the questions a final time, taking into consideration the new information they have from the pictures.

9 Conduct a whole-class discussion focusing on these questions:

- *Which gave you more information about the pictures—the subtitles, or the soundtrack?*

- *Which element—the subtitles, the soundtrack, or the pictures— gave you the most information about the story?*
- *Did anything on the soundtrack surprise you? What?*
- *Did anything in the pictures surprise you? What?*

VARIATION (for multilingual classes)

From captions to pictures. The activity as described above is only suitable for classes of students who share the same first language. However, for multilingual classes an interesting variation of this is possible using **closed-captioned** film clips instead of subtitled ones. Use an English-language film with closed-captions in English, and follow the same procedure described in steps 1–9 above, using the captions instead of subtitles. In the class discussion phase (step 9), ask the class to discuss the same questions, substituting the word 'captions' for 'subtitles'.

5.8 Hollywood style vs. national style

Students read an article and then compare Hollywood and their own national styles of filmmaking. In multinational classes students will choose their different national or regional cinemas (French, German, Japanese, Brazilian, African, etc.).

LEVEL

Upper-intermediate and above

TIME

30–60 minutes

MATERIALS

A copy of the article and worksheet for each student (see below).

PREPARATION

Prepare a photocopy of the article and the worksheet for each group of four students; prepare extra photocopies so that each student can have a copy later.

PROCEDURE

1 Divide the class into groups of four. Give each group a copy of the article.

2 Go over the article with the class. Deal with any comprehension or vocabulary problems.

3 Give each group a copy of the worksheet. Make sure the students understand all the questions on the worksheet. Hold the rest of the photocopies back so that you can distribute copies to individuals later.

4 Tell the groups to discuss and complete the worksheet.

5 As students work in their groups, copy the worksheet on the board. Leave a space for each group's results.

6 Elicit ideas from each group and mark the number of ticks on the board.

7 At the end of the activity, the class can agree on the characteristics of 'their' filmmaking styles compared to the 'Hollywood' filmmaking style.

ARTICLE

How Hollywood has changed

by Barry Tomalin

Since the original filmmakers moved from New York to Hollywood to exploit the quality of light in their filmmaking, Hollywood has changed a lot. People often say the classic Hollywood is the Hollywood of the 1920s to 40s, with the change from silent films to sound, and from black and white to colour. At this time Hollywood became dominated by the studio system in which a few major studios controlled the scripts, budgets, and directors of their films. They also controlled the distributions and marketing. There were only a few studios and a small group of companies controlled the cinema industry in America.

In the 50s the big studios began to decline as Television became stronger, and fewer people went to the cinema. Hollywood responded by producing 'big-scale' films with lots of action and excitement. These were often called 'blockbusters'. They had huge budgets and huge stars, and were shot in exotic locations that Television could not match.

In the 70s, with films like *Jaws* and *Star Wars*, Hollywood introduced **special effects** and Dolby digital sound systems, which increased the budget and created even more exotic situations and stories, often at the expense of character and plot. Many people said that Hollywood was only interested in the extremes of sex and violence and had lost interest in normal human stories.

In the 70s Hollywood also introduced the 'high concept' film, which relies on a big star such as Tom Cruise, and which makes use of pop music. This is then released as a soundtrack and bits of the film are then incorporated into pop videos.

A development of this in the 90s is the film which leads to sales of toys and, especially, computer games as well as cups, glasses, and clothes. Disney and Warner Brothers even have a chain of stores which are devoted to film merchandising.

This is not to say that no 'art' films are produced or distributed by studios. Some companies have specialised in art films, where plot and character are the key features. Miramax is a company which has had immense success with art films, especially *The English Patient*, which won the Oscar for best picture in 1997, although films such as *Batman*, *Indiana Jones*, or *The Lost World* are even more popular—but they don't win Oscars. Hollywood-style filmmaking dominates the world. How does it affect filmmaking where you are?

HOLLYWOOD STYLE VS. NATIONAL STYLE

A Which style of film (national or Hollywood) is stronger in each of the following elements? Tick the appropriate box.

	National	*Hollywood*
Storyline/plot	☐	☐
Character	☐	☐
Film stars	☐	☐
Location	☐	☐
Special effects	☐	☐
Music	☐	☐
Budget	☐	☐
Merchandising spin-offs (toys, computer games, etc.)	☐	☐

B Discuss these questions with your group and make notes on your answers.

1 Did your group base its conclusions on one national film or director? If so, which film or director?

2 Did your group base its conclusions on one Hollywood film or director? If so, which film or director?

3 In your group's opinion:

   a Are national films becoming more like Hollywood films?

   b Are national films exhibiting a national style and identity?

5.9 How have they changed?

Students watch original and dubbed versions of a clip and compare the voices of the actors.

Elementary and above

20–30 minutes

A clip of a film in its original language, and a **dubbed** version of the same film. Choose a film with a well-known film star with a distinctive voice. Harrison Ford and Michelle Pfeiffer are good examples. 'Mickey Mouse' animations where the characters have strong voices are also good. DVDs are good for this activity, as some contain the original soundtrack of the film, a soundtrack in a different language, and subtitles in one of the two languages (see the list of suggested DVDs); copies of the worksheet (see below).

WORSHEET

HOW HAVE THEY CHANGED?			
Character's name			
Voice qualities	*Silent version*	*Original version*	*Dubbed version*
High or low?			
Light or deep?			
Strong or weak?			
Sexy or prim?			
Hard or soft?			
Pleasant or unpleasant?			

How has the dubbing changed the character? ....

Is the dubbing more or less suitable for the film? ....

Is the dubbing more or less suitable for your culture? ....

PREPARATION

Make enough copies of the worksheet to give one to each student. Cue each film at the same point.

PROCEDURE

1 Distribute the worksheet. Go through it and make sure the students understand these words to describe voice quality: *high, low, light, deep, strong, weak, sexy, prim, hard, soft.* Depending on level of the students, you can introduce more descriptive words.

2 Explain the task. The students will see an actor on screen and decide what kind of voice they think he/she has.

3 Play the film clip of the original version, without sound. The students watch and fill in the worksheet.

4 Elicit ideas and write them on the board.

5 Play the film clip again, but this time with sound. The students fill in the worksheet with what they hear, and compare it with the appearance of the star on the screen, and make any changes they wish.

6 Now play the dubbed version. The students watch and listen, and make notes on the voice quality.

7 The students compare the dubbed voice and the original voice (which may also have been dubbed!). They discuss what effect the dubbed voice has had on:

• the character
• the film as a whole.

They then vote on whether the dubbed version is more or less convincing than the original.

VARIATION

At higher levels the students can discuss whether the dubbed voice is more appropriate for masculinity, femininity, strength, sexiness, etc. in their culture.

Some suggested DVDs to use with this activity:

Brief Encounter (1946)
Audio tracks: English, Italian
Subtitles: English

Casablanca (1943)
Audio tracks: English, French
Subtitles: English, French

The Cider House Rules (1999)
Soundtracks: English, French
Subtitles: English, Spanish

Cinema Paradiso (1990)
Audio tracks: Italian, English (dubbed)
Subtitles: English, Spanish, French, Italian

Das Boot (1982)
Audio tracks: German, English, Spanish
Subtitles: English, Spanish, French

Life is Beautiful (1998)
Audio tracks: Italian, English
  (dubbed)
Subtitles: English

Notting Hill (1999)
Audio tracks: English, French
Subtitles: English

The Sixth Sense (1999)
Audio tracks: English, French
Subtitles: English

The Sound of Music (1965)
Audio tracks: English, French
Subtitles: English, Spanish

Young Frankenstein (1974)
Audio tracks: English, French,
  Spanish
Subtitles: English

The Wizard of Oz (1939)
Audio tracks: English, French
Subtitles: English, French

5.10 Original vs. remake

Students view, discuss, and compare two versions of the same scene: the scene as it appears in the original version of the film, and the scene as it appears in the remake.

LEVEL

Intermediate and above

TIME

40–50 minutes

MATERIALS

Two clips of the same scene from two different versions of a film, for example, *Sabrina Fair* (1954) and *Sabrina* (1995), *The Shop Around the Corner* (1940) and *You've Got Mail* (1998), the 1968 and 1999 versions of *The Thomas Crown Affair*, *Death Takes a Holiday* (1934) and *Meet Joe Black* (1998), the 1960 and 1998 versions of *Psycho*, or *Frankenstein* (1931) and *Mary Shelley's Frankenstein* (1994); copies of the worksheet for each student (see below).

PREPARATION

Cue the film clips. Make enough copies of the worksheet to give one to each student.

PROCEDURE

1 Distribute the worksheet and explain the task to the students. They are going to watch two versions of the same scene from two different examples of a film: the original and the remake. They should watch each film clip and then use the worksheet to make notes about each version.

2 Play the film clip from the original version of the film. After playing the clip, allow students 5–10 minutes to make notes on their worksheets.

3 Repeat step 2 with the film clip from the remake.

4 Divide the class into groups of three or four.

5 Students use their worksheets as a basis for discussion of the two film clips.

6 Conduct a whole-class discussion centred on these questions:
- *What similarities did you notice between the two versions?*
- *What differences did you notice?*
- *Which version do you prefer? Why?*

FOLLOW-UP

Students can write a composition, in the lesson or as homework, using their completed worksheet as a guide, saying which version they liked better and why.

WORKSHEET

ORIGINAL vs. REMAKE		
	Original	*Remake*
Setting Time Place Situation		
Characters Sex Age Other		
Plot		
Emotions		

Photocopiable © Oxford University Press

5.11 What's the title?

Students translate film titles from their first language into English.

LEVEL

Intermediate and above

TIME

20–30 minutes

MATERIALS

A selection of 8–10 film titles or film advertisements for British, American, or Commonwealth films in the students' first language(s), see sample worksheet below.

PREPARATION

For each film title you select, find out the title in English. You can do this at either of the following websites:
Empire Magazine: http://www.empireonline.co.uk
The Internet Movie Database: http://www.imdb.com

PROCEDURE

1 Ask the class to work in small groups.

2 Write up on the board the titles in the first language, or distribute them round the class (one or two titles per group).

3 Explain the task. The groups must translate the film titles into English and create a stylish English title for each.

4 Each group translates its title or titles and then passes it to another group. Each group should translate a total of eight to ten titles.

5 Each group takes its translations and tries to make them more stylish, for example:

- French: *La Guerre des Etoiles*
- literal translation: *The War of the Stars*
- stylish title: *Star Wars*.

6 Elicit the English titles from the groups. The groups decide which English version of each title they prefer.

7 Finally, show the real title in English. The class compare their versions with the English title.

VARIATION 1

If you wish, students can take English film titles and translate them into their first language.

VARIATION 2

Students could match titles in their first language with English titles, or vice versa (see sample worksheet).

ANSWER KEY

1 g, 2 j, 3 a, 4 b, 5 i, 6 c, 7 d, 8 e, 9 f, 10 h

SAMPLE WORKSHEET

MATCH THE TITLES	
French titles	*English titles*
1 La Guerre des Étoiles	a House on Haunted Hill
2 Miss Daisy et son chauffeur	b From Dusk till Dawn
3 Maison de l'horreur	c Jaws
4 Une nuit en enfer	d Being John Malkovich
5 Une histoire vraie	e A Nightmare on Elm Street
6 Les dents de la mer	f Hollow Man
7 Dans la peau de John Malkovich	g Star Wars
8 Les griffes de la nuit	h The Horse Whisperer
9 L'homme sans ombre	i The Straight Story
10 L'homme qui murmurait à l'oreille des chevaux	j Driving Miss Daisy

5.12 Drama vs. documentary

Students watch and compare a clip from a film drama based on a true story with a film or television documentary version of the same story.

LEVEL

Intermediate and above

TIME

30–60 minutes

MATERIALS

A film clip from a drama based on a true story and a clip from a television or film **documentary** based on the same story, for example, the drama *JFK* (1991) and the documentary *Beyond 'JFK': The Question of Conspiracy* (1992). If a documentary is not available, use a newspaper article that tells the story.

PREPARATION

Cue each video at the point where there is a difference between the drama and the documentary story. Choose points where the two versions present the same event or series of events, but where there are obvious differences, for example, in the names, ages or sexes of the people involved, the places where the events take place, the time in which the events take place, or the order of the events themselves.

PROCEDURE

1 Explain the task. The students must watch the film and compare it with the documentary evidence.

2 Show the film clip. The students make notes on what happens.

3 Elicit the information from the class.

4 Write the following headings on the board if they are relevant:
   - *Name*
   - *Age*
   - *Sex*
   - *Place*
   - *Time*
   - *Events*
   - *Other*

5 Play the documentary clip. The students note any differences from the film using the headings in step 4.

6 Elicit the differences from the class.

VARIATION

Instead of a documentary film, use a newspaper or magazine article about the story on which the film drama is based.

6 Focusing on characters

Characterization is a key feature of literary study, and this is no less true of film. The character-based activities in this chapter allow students to practise the language of description along with the four skills of listening, speaking, reading, and writing.

'Character posters' (6.3) invites students to use pictures and creative writing to present information about film characters in the form of 'Missing' or 'Wanted' posters of their own design. In 'Character sketches' (6.4) and 'Character webs' (6.5) students work individually to summarize information about characters and then get together in groups to compare and discuss their ideas. In 'Comparing characters' (6.6) students use a Venn diagram to compare two characters in a film, and then write a composition comparing the two characters. In 'Focus on characters' behaviour' (6.8) and 'Who's who?' (6.9), students view film clips and then get together in groups to analyse and discuss the personality traits and behaviour of selected characters.

Some activities encourage students to communicate 'directly' with characters. In 'Character interviews' (6.2) students have a chance to role-play a press conference in which reporters interview characters from a film or film clip they have seen. In 'Dear film friend' (6.7) students practise writing skills by composing personal letters to film characters of their choice.

Finally, in 'Cartoons' (6.1), students practise reading and viewing skills by comparing the exploits of well-known comic strip characters with the way they are **portrayed** on film.

6.1 Cartoons

Students compare comic strip and film versions of a cartoon.

LEVEL

Intermediate and above

TIME

20–30 minutes

MATERIALS

A comic strip of a cartoon; a clip from a film adaptation based on the same cartoon, for example, *Superman: the Movie* (1978) starring Christopher Reeve as Superman, compared to *Superman* (Marvel Comics); copies of the worksheet for each student (see below).

WORKSHEET

CARTOON STRIPS		
	Print version	*Film version*
Characters Are there any differences in the number or names of the main characters?		
Dress What differences do you notice in the way the characters are dressed?		
Behaviour What differences do you notice in the behaviour of the main characters?		
Location What differences do you notice in the location?		
'Goodies' and 'baddies' Is there a difference in behaviour of the goodies and baddies?		
Colours Is there a difference in the colours used in the cartoon pictures and the film?		
Storyline Are there differences in the storyline?		
Ending What differences do you see in the end of the scene or scenes you watched?		
Can you suggest any reasons for the differences you noted?		

PREPARATION   Make enough copies of the comic strip and the worksheet to give one to each student; cue the film clip (the film storyline doesn't have to be the same as that of the print version, but it will help if it is similar).

PROCEDURE   1 Pre-teach the following words:

- *cartoon*
- *comic strip*
- the English names of some popular cartoon characters, for example, *Popeye, Superman, Wonderwoman, Batman*.

2 Distribute the comic strip and go over it with the students. At this point you could get the students to act out the dialogue and storyline.

3 Distribute the worksheet, and tell the students that you are going to play a film clip based on the comic strip they have just read. Their task is to watch the film clip, compare it with the comic strip, and then complete the worksheet by writing down any differences.

4 Go over the worksheet with the students to make sure they understand the questions.

5 Play the film clip.

6 The students work alone, completing their worksheets.

7 When students have finished filling in their worksheets, divide the class into groups of three or four. Groups discuss the questions on the worksheet and compare answers.

8 Get the class to vote on which version they prefer, and get student volunteers to say why.

FOLLOW-UP   Conduct a whole-class discussion of this question: *Which famous cartoon characters have not been made into films?* (for example, *Andy Capp* or *Rupert Bear*). *Why not?*

6.2 Character interviews

Students roleplay a press conference in which reporters interview characters from a film.

LEVEL   **Intermediate and above**

TIME   **40–60 minutes**

MATERIALS   None

PREPARATION   None, except that all the students need to have seen the same film or film clip.

PROCEDURE

1 Tell students they are going to have a chance to interview some characters from the film or film clip they have seen. Ask the class to suggest some characters they would like to interview. Write the names of the suggested characters on the board. If characters are not actually named in the film or film clip, they can be identified by a description, for example, 'the man with the dog'.

2 Divide the class into groups of 4–6 students.

3 Explain the task to the students. From the list on the board, groups choose a character they want to interview. Half the group should write questions for the interviewer, and the other half should discuss how the character would behave in an interview, what questions might he/she be asked, and how he/she might respond to them. Then each group should choose two people from their group to act out the interview for the whole class.

4 Students work in groups, preparing for the interviews.

5 Students from the groups take turns roleplaying the interviews.

6 After each roleplay, discuss the interview as a class. Use the following questions to guide the discussion:

- *What adjectives would you use to describe the character's behaviour?*
- *What adjectives would you use to describe the interviewer's behaviour?*
- *What adjectives would you use to describe the interviewer's questions?*
- *In your opinion, what was the most interesting part of the interview?*

VARIATION

Press conference: Student volunteers prepare the roles of characters while the rest of the class prepare questions for reporters to ask the characters. Then, the characters stand or sit in front of the class. Reporters ask the characters their questions.

6.3 Character posters

Students design 'Missing' or 'Wanted' posters for film characters.

LEVEL

Elementary and above

TIME

40–50 minutes

MATERIALS

Drawing materials including paper and coloured pens, pencils, or crayons; sample poster (see below).

Missing

Name:	Dorothy Gale
Age:	12
Height:	4'11"
Weight:	95 lbs
Eyes:	Hazel
Hair:	Brown

Dorothy left her aunt and uncle's farm during a twister. She and her dog Toto were last seen skipping along the yellow brick road in the direction of Emerald City. She was wearing ruby slippers and a blue checked pinafore. If you have any information, please contact Auntie Em and Uncle Henry in Kansas.

PROCEDURE

1 Explain the task to the students. They are going to design a 'Missing' or 'Wanted' poster for a character in a film they have seen.

2 Ask the students to suggest the kind of information that is usually found on such posters. Student ideas are likely to include the following:

- the character's name
- age
- height
- weight
- hair colour
- eye colour
- the person's home address
- where they were last seen
- what they were wearing
- who they were seen with
- who to contact with information
- the reward, if any.

3 Students work individually or in groups to design their posters.

FOLLOW-UP

Display the posters in the classroom.

REMARKS

'Missing' and 'Wanted' posters are a very entertaining way of getting students to summarize information about a character whose whereabouts are unknown by another character, or who is in trouble with the law. Detective films, mysteries, and thrillers lend themselves very easily to this activity, but less obvious choices can produce amusing results, for example, the sample poster inspired by *The Wizard of Oz*.

6.4 Character sketches

Students choose a character from a short story, graded reader, children's book, fairy tale, folk tale, or nursery rhyme, and write a character sketch.

LEVEL

Intermediate and above

TIME

40–50 minutes

MATERIALS

Copies of the worksheet (see below).

PREPARATION

Make enough copies of the worksheet to give one to each student.

PROCEDURE

1 Tell the class to imagine the film version of a well-known character in a short story, graded reader, or children's story, for example, *Cinderella*. Ask the class: *What things do you need to think about in order to make the characters in the film as accurate, interesting, and enjoyable as they are in the original story?*

2 Distribute the worksheet. Explain to the students that they should choose a favourite character from a children's book, fairy tale, or nursery rhyme as the subject of a character sketch. They may choose the same characters or different characters from the same story. They can also choose different stories. Students should use the worksheet to write down their ideas about the character they chose.

3 Students work alone, completing the items on the worksheet.

4 Divide the class into groups of three or four. Groups work together, asking each other questions about their characters and then comparing and discussing their character sketches.

WORKSHEET

CHARACTER SKETCH

Name of story: ....

Name of character: ....

Physical appearance What does the character look like? Are these physical features important in understanding the character? If so, why?	
Actions What does the character do in the story? How do these actions affect the viewer's understanding of the character?	
Interactions with other characters How does this character interact with other characters in the story? What do these reactions reveal about the character?	
Motivation What does the character think about the situations around him or her? How do the character's thoughts affect what we know about the character?	

Photocopiable © Oxford University Press

FOLLOW-UP

VARIATION

Each student creates a casting list of actors and actresses they feel could play the main characters in a film version of their chosen story. In a future class, students can create film posters or other advertisements for their film version of a children's story. (See 1.7, 'Film posters', on page 21.)

Ask students to imagine themselves as a character in a film and to develop a character description of themselves. Finally, they list three actors or actresses and discuss why each actor would be a good choice to play them.

6.5 Character webs

Students use a character web to describe a character in a film they have seen.

LEVEL

Lower-intermediate and above

TIME

20–30 minutes

MATERIALS

A character web for each student (see below).

PREPARATION

Make enough copies of the character web to give one to each student.

PROCEDURE

1 Distribute the character webs and tell the students they are going to use them to describe one of the characters in the film.

2 Assign a character to each student and explain the task. They should:

- write the name of their character in the circle in the centre of the web.
- label each of the four larger circles with a word that describes the character, for example, *good, generous, intelligent, charismatic.*
- make notes that support the descriptions, for example, the character's own words or actions, or the words or actions of other characters.

3 Students work alone, completing their webs.

4 When students have finished their webs, divide the class into groups of three or four. Each member of the group should have a different character.

5 Write the following questions on the board:

- *Do you agree with the description? Why or why not?*
- *What are your own ideas about the character?*
- *What other words would you use to describe the character?*

6 In their groups, students take turns describing their characters, based on the information in the webs. Group members listen to each description and then use the questions on the board as a basis for discussion of each character.

FOLLOW-UP

Students use the information in their character webs to write a composition describing the character.

WORKSHEET

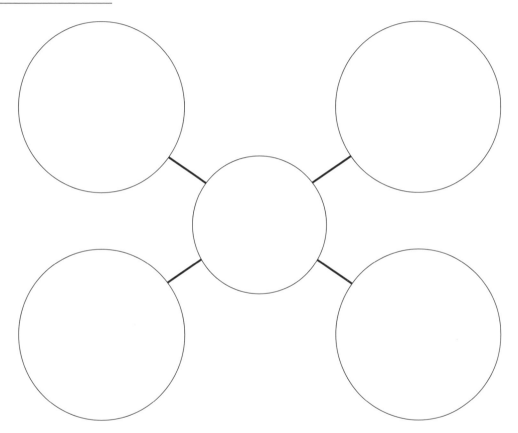

6.6 Comparing characters

Students use a Venn diagram to compare two characters in a film. They then use the information in the diagram to write a composition about the characters.

LEVEL

Lower-intermediate and above

TIME

15–20 minutes + time to write the composition in class or at home

MATERIALS   Venn diagrams samples (see below).

PREPARATION   None, but students need to have seen a film or a film clip with enough information to compare and contrast two characters in the manner described below.

PROCEDURE   1 After watching the film or film clip, draw a Venn diagram on the board or on an overhead transparency.

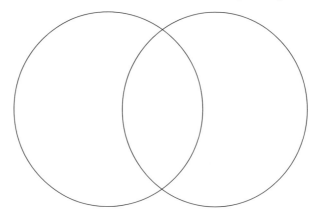

In the circle on the left, write the name of one of characters to be compared. In the circle on the right, write the name of the other character. In the place where the circles overlap, write *Both*.

2 Explain the task to the students. They are going to use the diagram to compare two characters in the film, and then use the information in the diagram to write a composition about the characters.

3 Ask the class questions to elicit information about the characters, for example:

- *What kind of person is X?*
- *What kind of person is Y?*
- *How are the characters alike?*
- *How are they different?*

As student volunteers respond, write key words from their answers in the appropriate section of the diagram.

4 Students use the information in the completed diagram to write a composition in which they compare the two characters.

FOLLOW-UP   After students become familiar with the Venn diagram technique, steps 1–3 of this activity can be done by students working individually, in pairs, or in small groups.

VARIATION 1   Students can compare three or more characters by using a Venn diagram with three or more overlapping circles.

VARIATION 2

Students can choose the two characters they want to compare. Assign students who have chosen the same characters to work together in groups of three or four.

REMARKS

In addition to being a useful tool for comparing characters in a film (see the example, which was inspired by the characters Miss Daisy and Hoke in *Driving Miss Daisy*), the Venn diagram technique can be used to compare features, such as plot and setting, in different films. Students might, for example, compare the balcony scene in any of the numerous film versions of *Romeo and Juliet* with the balcony scene in *West Side Story*.

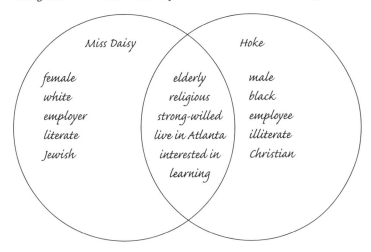

6.7 Dear film friend

Students write a letter to a character in a film.

LEVEL

Elementary and above

TIME

50–60 minutes

MATERIALS

None

PREPARATION

None, but students need to have seen the same film or film clip. Films with strong characterization, for example, dramas, biographies, or documentaries, work best for this activity.

PROCEDURE

1 (Optional) If the students are unfamiliar with the English format for letter writing, review basic letter-writing with the class.

2 Tell students they are going to write a letter to a character from the film or film clip they have seen. Their task is to choose a character, and then write a letter to him/her.

3 Ask the class to name some of the characters they might write to. As volunteers respond, write the names of the characters on the board.

4 Ask individual students to choose the character they would like to write to. Then divide the class into small groups, each group composed of students who have selected the same character.

5 Ask groups to brainstorm some questions they might want to raise about their chosen character. Depending on the class, you may want to suggest some of the following questions as a starting point. Remind the students they are writing about the character, not the actor who plays him/her.

- *What do you like or admire about the character?*
- *What do you dislike about the character?*
- *Why does the character interest you?*
- *What do you (the writer) and the character have in common?*
- *What advice, if any, do you have for the character?*
- *What are the character's plans for the future?*

6 Tell students to work individually and write a personal letter to the character of their choice.

7 When students have finished writing their letters, get them to exchange letters with a partner. Students read the letters, imagine they are the character the letter is addressed to and, as a homework assignment, write a response to the sender.

FOLLOW-UP

In the next lesson, students work in small groups, reading aloud the letters they received in the previous lesson, and the letters they have written in response.

VARIATION

Character to character: Students imagine themselves as a character in a film and write a letter to another character in the same film. They give clues and describe their actions. Get students to read their letters aloud or post the letters around the room. Students have to guess which film character wrote each letter.

6.8 Focus on characters' behaviour

Students view a film clip, choose a character, make notes, and then work in groups, discussing their chosen characters.

LEVEL

Intermediate and above

TIME

30–45 minutes

MATERIALS

A film clip featuring several characters in a situation that will encourage discussion about the characters' personalities and behaviour.

PREPARATION	Cue the film clip.

PROCEDURE

1 Write the following questions on the board:

- *What's the most important thing the character does in the scene?*
- *Do you like or dislike the character?*
- *What are the character's good points?*
- *What are his or her bad points?*
- *Would you act the same way in the same situation?*
- *If not, what would you do differently?*

2 Tell the students they are going to watch a scene with several characters. Their task is to focus on one character and make notes to answer the questions on the board. Tell the students the general nature of the scene, and identify the various characters. Divide the students into pairs or small groups and allocate a character to each group.

3 Play the film clip twice. Allow students time to make notes after each time they watch.

4 Groups discuss their chosen character, using the questions on the board.

5 Groups take turns reporting to the class. A spokesperson from each group summarizes the group's discussion.

FOLLOW-UP

Students use the questions as a starting point for writing a short composition about a chosen character. They then get together in groups and read their compositions to one another.

6.9 Who's who?

Students watch a film clip, make notes about the main characters, and then share the information they have gathered.

LEVEL

Upper-elementary and above

TIME

20–30 minutes

MATERIALS

A worksheet for each student (see below); a clip from an early part of a film, in which the main characters are established, for example, the opening sequence of *Kramer vs. Kramer,* in which we see shots of (1) Ted Kramer (played by Dustin Hoffman) at his job in an advertising agency; (2) his wife, Joanna, (Meryl Streep) putting their child, Billy, to bed; (3) Ted realizing its late and rushing home from his job; and (4) Joanna packing her travel kit.

PREPARATION

Make enough copies of the worksheet to give one copy to each student (or two if more than three main characters are introduced); cue the film clip.

PROCEDURE

1 If necessary, pre-teach the following vocabulary items:
   - *character* (a person in a story)
   - *clip* (a short section of a film)
   - *personality* (the distinctive nature and qualities of a person)
   - *physical description* (what someone looks like: hair colour, height, body type, etc.)
   - *role* (the part someone plays in a story).

2 Divide the class into groups made up of the same number of students as there are main characters in the film sequence.

3 Distribute the worksheet and tell the students that they are going to see a film clip twice. As they watch the first time, each person in their group should focus on a different character. The second time they watch, they should use the boxes on the worksheet to fill in the information about the character.

4 Identify the different characters in the clip, for example, 'Character 1 is the woman in the red dress', and write this information on the board. Then ask groups to divide up the characters so that each member of the group is a different character.

5 Play the clip twice. The first time, the students watch. The second time, they watch and make notes.

6 Students work in their groups, sharing and discussing the information they have noted about the characters. Each student completes the worksheet with information about *all* the characters.

7 Play the clip a third time. Students watch and check the information on their worksheets.

FOLLOW-UP

You can ask students to choose one character that interests them and write an imaginary biography of him/her, perhaps for homework. In lower-level classes, students may find it helpful if you provide them with a list of questions to use as a starting-point for writing the biographies, for example:

- *What is the character's name?*
- *Where and when was he/she born?*
- *Where did he/she grow up?*
- *What was his/her childhood like?*

VARIATION

With more advanced-level classes, individual students can be asked to make notes about *all* of the main characters in a clip. In this case, you may want to pause the film at points where there is a good shot of one or several main characters to give students more time to think and write about the characters.

REMARKS

With lower-level classes, you may want to model the activity, on the board or on an overhead projector, by working with the class to fill out the information about one of the characters.

WORKSHEET

	WHO'S WHO?		

Watch the film clip and fill in the information about each character.

	Character 1	Character 2	Character 3
Name			
Role			
Sex			
Age			
Job			
Physical Description			
Personality			

Photocopiable © Oxford University Press

7 Project work

This chapter focuses on ongoing activities that can be extended, and organized projects that can engage groups of learners over a period of time. Some, for example, 'Developing film treatments' (7.1), provide opportunities for incorporating activities from other chapters. Most of the activities require work in small groups, and many encourage personal involvement by allowing students to give concrete expression to their personal ideas through student-led tasks.

Ongoing activities include 'Film journals' (7.3) and 'Film presentations' (7.4). These are repeated classroom activities, like book reports in literature classes. In 'Film journals' students give personal responses to specific questions, or write freely about films they have seen. 'Film presentations' asks groups of students to work together to create and carry out structured presentations on films of their own choosing. Both of these activities, 'Film journals' and 'Film presentations', encourage students to bring their personal ideas, opinions, and out-of-school lives into the classroom.

Excellent opportunities for whole-class and group projects are offered by 'Developing film treatments' (7.1), 'Film guides' (7.2), 'Make a movie magazine' (7.6), and 'Make your own trailer' (7.7). These activities encourage students to think up ideas for films, compile their own movie guide newspaper column, create a classroom magazine devoted to film, and to plan, storyboard, and even use video to create trailers for films they have seen.

For teachers who would like their classes to study a complete film as a classroom project over, say, a week or a term, 'Film viewing project' (7.5) outlines the steps in the process.

7.1 Developing film treatments

Students create film treatments based on characters and settings chosen at random.

LEVEL
Upper-intermediate and above

TIME
At least two 50-minute lessons (plus homework)

MATERIALS
A hat or bag.

PREPARATION
Prepare two sheets of paper for each group.

PROCEDURE

Lesson 1

1 Introduce the noun *treatment* (a written summary of a film that shows how the writer would 'treat' the story in a screenplay). Explain to the students that in the first lesson they will be creating their own film treatments, with one catch—they will be using characters and settings suggested by other groups of students and picked from a paper bag or hat.

2 Divide the class into groups of three or four. Ask each group to imagine two different characters and write a short description of them, each on a different sheet of paper. Each description should include the character's name, age, occupation, and two or three of the character's lifetime goals.

3 Tell students to fold the pieces of paper in half. Collect them all and put them in the hat or bag.

4 Each group pulls two characters from the hat or bag, who will then become the main characters in their film.

5 Each group writes down a setting (a location and time period) where the film will take place, for example, London in the year 2099.

6 As with the character descriptions, these papers with the settings should be folded in half and placed in the hat or bag, then drawn by each group, and the setting selected will become the setting of the group's film.

   NOTE: Do not allow groups to change characters or setting with other groups. The most unusual combinations often result in the funniest and most interesting plots.

7 Each group uses the remaining class time to discuss how the characters they have picked might interact in the chosen setting, making notes on their ideas for later use.

Homework

Using their selected characters and setting, each group creates a film 'treatment'. Groups write a two- to three-page description, in simple descriptive language or in outline form, describing how the characters will behave in the setting, and summarizing important details of the plot. Groups should also create a title for their film.

Lesson 2

8 Groups take turns presenting their film treatment to the class in order to sell their project. This is called 'pitching your project'.

9 The class vote on which film treatment they like best.

FOLLOW-UP

The class develops some scenes for the best treatment by working in small groups to create scripts for the characters in the setting described. (See 3.9, 'Writing film scripts', on page 75.)

7.2 Film guides

Students examine the style and techniques of a newspaper-style 'film guide' and then write their own brief summaries of films they have seen.

LEVEL

Intermediate and above

TIME

2 lessons

MATERIALS

A sample film guide for each student (see below).

PREPARATION

Make enough copies of the sample film guide below to give one to each student, or use copies of a recent film guide from an English-language newspaper.

PROCEDURE

Lesson 1

1 Warm up the class by asking students the following question: *What elements make up a film?* As students respond, under the heading 'Film elements', list key words from their answers on the board, for example, *plot, acting, music,* **cinematography**, *characters, setting, direction.* Do not erase the words, as the list will be helpful to students later in the activity.

2 Give one copy of the sample film guide to each student.

3 Get the class to read and discuss 3–4 of the short film reviews in the film guide. Include at least one film that received a bad review. For each review, conduct a whole-class discussion based on the following questions:

- *What is the plot of this film?*
- *In what genre (drama, comedy, documentary, horror, science fiction, etc.) could this film be classified?*
- *What is the reviewer's opinion of the actors' performances?*
- *What descriptive words show the reviewer's opinions of the acting, plot, and other film elements?*
- *Had you heard of this film before reading this review? If so, does the review change your opinion of the film? Why or why not?*
- *Does this review encourage you to see the film? Why or why not?*

4 Explain to the students that they are each going to write a mini-review of a film they have seen. Ask each student to select a film, either an old favourite or one currently playing in a cinema, for the focus of a short (100–150 words) film review similar to those in the sample film guide. Make sure that each student selects a different film.

5 Direct students' attention to the list of 'Film elements' drawn up in Step 1. Elicit suggestions for additional elements that

should be included in their film reviews. The final list should include the following:

- names of actors starring in the film
- name of the director
- length of film
- evaluation of the plot
- evaluation of the actors' performances
- any elements that make this film unique (for example, soundtrack, cinematography, etc.)
- use of descriptive language.

6 Ask students to 'pre-write' their mini-reviews in class. Remind them that their reviews should contain between 100–150 words.

Homework

Students write their film reviews.

Lesson 2

1 Divide the class into groups of three or four. Students take turns reading their reviews to their group. Group members discuss the review and make suggestions for editing.

2 Students work individually, rewriting final copies of their reviews.

3 Collect all the reviews and display them on a classroom bulletin board under the heading 'Film guide'. Allow students class time to examine all the reviews. Alternatively, you may choose to ask the students to assemble all their reviews in a 'Film guide' column for the school newspaper.

FOLLOW-UP

As an extension of this activity, the class can discuss these questions:

- *How do movie reviews influence whether or not people see a film?*
- *How are film reviews different from other types of newspaper article?*
- *What makes certain films popular? Why?*
- *In your opinion, what makes a 'good' film?*
- *How are films rated? In your opinion, are these rating systems effective?*
- *What different people are involved in the creation of a film, and what do they do?*

VARIATION 1

Get students to examine newspaper advertisements for films and then create their own advertisements for favourite films. Remind students to emphasize important film elements such as character, plot, setting, mood, and other aspects.

VARIATION 2

In more advanced classes, students can compare the reviews in the film guide to longer reviews and discuss: *What are the similarities and differences?*

VARIATION 3

Let students see one of the films reviewed in the sample film guide and ask them to write reviews in response to the one offered in the film guide, agreeing or disagreeing with the points it makes. (See 4.5, 'Writing film reviews', page 84.)

SAMPLE FILM GUIDE

FILM GUIDE

Here is a selected list of movies playing in local cinemas this weekend. An asterisk (*) signifies a highly-recommended film. Running times are in parentheses.

Now playing

* ***Antz,*** starring the voices of Woody Allen, Sharon Stone, and Gene Hackman. Directed by Eric Darnell, Lawrence Guterman, and Tim Johnson (79 minutes). In this entertaining computer-animated feature set in an ant colony, neurotic worker ant Z (voice of Woody Allen) strives to reconcile his own individuality with the communal work-ethic of the colony. He falls in love with the queen ant's daughter, Princess Bala (voice of Sharon Stone) and when the entire worker population is threatened by termites and the evil General Mandible (voice of Gene Hackman), he must save the ant colony. Themes of individuality run rampant in this clever, enjoyable, and sophisticated comedy.

Battlefield Earth, starring John Travolta, Barry Pepper, and Forest Whitaker. Directed by Roger Christian (117 minutes). In this film, based on the novel by L. Ron Hubbard, a race of business-minded aliens called Psychlos attempt to conquer the Earth in the year 3000. All that is left of humanity are slaves and ignorant savages. One of the most powerful leaders on Earth is Psychlo Chief of Security. Terl (John Travolta) has a plan to exploit Earth's human slaves, but what he doesn't know is that one bright human, Jonnie Goodboy Tyler (Barry Pepper), is about to spoil his plan. The confused plot, leaden pace, intrusive musical score, and Travolta's hammy performance combine to present an incredibly dull picture of the future of humanity.

* ***The Bounty***, starring Mel Gibson, Anthony Hopkins, Laurence Olivier, and Daniel Day Lewis. Directed by Roger Donaldson (130 minutes). This beautiful, well-made film retells the story of the mutiny on the HMS *Bounty* near Polynesia the 1700s. The tale is told in a series of flashbacks as Captain William Bligh (Anthony Hopkins) answers questions before a naval review board in London. Of all the Bounty films perhaps this one presents the most accurate description of what happened between Captain Bligh and his friend Fletcher Christian (Mel Gibson). Hopkins gives a powerful, well-rounded characterization of Bligh, but Gibson's portrayal of Christian lacks real substance. Arthur Ibbetson's cinematography is noteworthy, and the soundtrack by Vangelis is wonderfully haunting.

* ***Bride of Frankenstein***, starring Boris Karloff, Colin Clive, Ernest Thesiger, and Elsa Lanchester. Directed by James Whale (75 minutes). This audacious and wild sequel to *Frankenstein* is even better than its predecessor. A rich vein of dry wit runs through the chills as the weird Dr. Pretorius (Ernest Thesiger) forces Dr. Henry Frankenstein (Colin Clive) to create a 'bride' (Elsa Lanchester) for the Monster (Boris Karloff). Highlights of this highly entertaining horror film include the pastoral interlude with the blind hermit and the final, riotous creation scene. A highly entertaining script by John L. Balderston and William Hurlbut, along with Franz Waxman's marvellous score make this a must-see, classic thriller.

* ***Buena Vista Social Club***, starring Ry Cooder, Ruben Gonzalez, Ibrahim Ferrer, and Compay Segundo. Directed by Wim Wenders (104 minutes). In this exceptional documentary film a group of legendary Cuban musicians are brought together by guitarist Ry Cooder to record a CD. The film presents actual scenes from recording sessions in Havana and features on-camera interviews in which the ageing musicians, some in their nineties, talk about their lives in Cuba and how they got started in music. The film includes exciting live footage of a reunion concert in Amsterdam and affectionate scenes of the musicians' journey to New York's Carnegie Hall. Music from the Grammy award-winning CD produced by Ry Cooder is used on the soundtrack.

In Love and War, starring Chris O'Donnell and Sandra Bullock. Directed by Richard Attenborough (115 minutes). This period drama is the story of the relationship between Ernest Hemingway and Agnes von Kurowsky, the inspiration behind Hemingway's novel *A Farewell to Arms*. The story begins in First World War Italy when ambulance driver Hemingway (Chris O'Donnell) is injured and ends up in hospital. There he meets and falls in love with his nurse, Agnes von Kurowsky (Sandra Bullock). This slow-moving film recounts their ill-fated romance through to its conclusion after the war. Flat and uninteresting location shots, stiff and plodding direction, and a total lack of chemistry between the two **leads** make this one of the most boring films of the decade.

Notting Hill, starring Julia Roberts, Hugh Grant, Richard McCabe, and Rhys Ifans. Directed by Roger Mitchell (123 minutes). In this romantic comedy the life of Will Thacker (Hugh Grant), a simple London bookshop owner, changes when he accidentally meets Anna Scott (Julia Roberts), a world-famous film star. Love immediately blossoms, but fame and Anna's American movie star boyfriend (played by Alec Baldwin) get in the way. While the film is not without its funny moments, mainly in the performance of Rhys Ifans as Will's messy flatmate Spike, the story is totally predictable and the relationship between the main characters feels forced. The best thing about this film is the supporting cast, an interesting group of characters who are more likeable and believable than the leads.

* ***A Room with a View***, starring Maggie Smith, Helena Bonham Carter, and Denholm Elliott. Directed by James Ivory (117 minutes). This elegant and witty adaptation of E. M. Forster's novel about Lucy Honeychurch (Helena Bonham Carter), a young girl visiting Italy at the turn of the century, won Oscars for screenplay adaptation (Ruth

Prawer Jhabvala), art direction, and costume design, but the best thing about this film is the acting. Daniel Day-Lewis is particularly good as Cecil Vyse, Lucy's rejected fiancé. Excellent work is also done by Maggie Smith as Lucy's poor cousin Charlotte, Denholm Elliott as the free-thinking Mr. Emerson, and Judi Dench as the romantic novelist Miss Lavish. This intelligent, beautifully-made film, full of humour and passion, is a treat for the eyes, ears, mind, and heart.

7.3 Film journals

Students keep journals about films they have seen.

LEVEL	**Elementary and above**
TIME	**5–10 minutes a day**
MATERIALS	A guide for writing a film journal for each student (see sample below).
PREPARATION	Make enough copies of the guide to give one to each student; make sure each student has a notebook to use as a film journal.
PROCEDURE	1 Tell the students that they are going to keep a film journal. Explain that the purpose of the journal is to give them a chance to write about any films they see.

2 Distribute the guide, and explain that it is a guide for writing about any films or film clips they have seen. Tell them they may want to paste it inside the front cover of their journals to remind them of the some of the ways they can write about films. Tell them that they don't just have to use the topics suggested in the guide. The only requirements are that they write about all the films they see, and that they write as much as they can.

3 Go over the information in the guide to be sure students understand what they have to do. Remind them that they should write in their film journals every time they see a film, whether they watch it in the lesson, at home, or in a cinema.

Ideas for using journals

a In addition to giving students plenty of opportunities to write freely about films they have seen, you can also give them some journal assignments. For example, you might ask students to write a response to one or several of the following questions:

- *Which character in the film would you most like to meet? What would you say to him or her? How do you think the character would respond?*
- *Which character would you least like to meet and talk to? Why?*

- *Which character in the film would you most like to play? Why?*
- *Do you know anyone like one of the characters in the film? Write about how this person is similar to, and different from, the character in the film.*

b Volunteers can select a part of their journal entry that they particularly like and read it aloud to the whole class.

c Instead of writing their journal entries in the lesson, students can write them as homework and hand in their notebooks for the teacher to read every week.

d Ask pairs of students to exchange journals to see and discuss what each has written.

e After writing in their journals, students can get together in groups of four or five and take turns reading their journal entries aloud to the members of the group.

REMARKS

This activity is best done as a fluency activity. The goal is to get students used to the idea of writing regularly and a lot. Students will write more when they are given positive feedback on the amount and creativity of their writing. Too much criticism of grammar, spelling, and so on may discourage students from writing. Make a point of collecting and reading students' journals at least once a week. When reading and responding to journal entries, be sure to include a positive comment about the student's work. You may find it useful to use the '2 plus 1' technique, two positive comments and one opportunity for improvement. In this case the opportunity for improvement could be a grammar or vocabulary point.

If the students request correction of grammar and vocabulary, feel free to do so.

GUIDE TO WRITING YOUR FILM JOURNAL

Every time that you see a film clip or a whole film—in the lesson, at home, or in a cinema—you should write about the film in a special notebook that you keep only as a journal. You can describe what you have seen and heard on the film, give your opinion of it, say what you know about the actors or director (or anything else associated with the film), compare it to another film or other films you have seen, say what the film reminds you of, or write about how the film makes you feel and why it makes you feel that way. Write as much as you can. The important thing is to write a lot about the film you have seen and not worry about correct spelling or grammar.

7.4 Film presentations

Students make structured presentations about films they have seen.

LEVEL   **Intermediate and above**

TIME   **Part of several lessons (plus extra-curricular time)**

MATERIALS   (Optional) A worksheet for each student (see below).

PREPARATION   (Optional) Make enough copies of the worksheet to give one to each student.

PROCEDURE   **Lesson 1**

1 (Optional) Distribute the worksheet and tell them to follow the instructions.

2 Divide the class into groups of 3–5 students. Explain the task to the students. Each group will choose and watch a film in their own time outside of lesson time and:

- write a one-page written synopsis for the rest of the students
- decide on four main scenes for study by the class.

3 Give each group a different presentation day when they can talk about their film to the class. Tell the groups they will each have 25–30 minutes for their presentations.

Lesson 2+ (presentation days)

4 The group announces they are going to present a film and tells the title to the class. They distribute the synopsis to the class.

5 Class members read the synopsis and ask the group any comprehension questions.

6 The group presents their four scenes one by one. For each scene, they explain:

- what happens in the scene
- why it is important and why they chose it
- what the class should look for in terms of:
  - plot development
  - character development
  - design features
  - writing and acting.

7 Following the presentation, class members ask questions and discuss their reactions to the film and the presentation.

8 Follow up each presentation by giving feedback on your view of the film and the language used by the presenters.

REMARKS

When students prepare and present this work themselves under your guidance, it often results in a far greater degree of class involvement and discussion than teacher-led activities.

WORKSHEET

FILM PRESENTATIONS

Work in a group of 3–5 students. Together with the people in your group, do the following:

Preparation

Before your presentation day:

Choose a film and watch it in your own time, outside of the lesson. Decide on 3–5 scenes which you think are important to show the class. There should be one scene for each member of the group. Write a one-page synopsis of the film for the lesson (this will give the information missing from the scenes).
Make enough copies of the synopsis to give one to each student.

Presentation Day

Your group should be prepared to:

- tell the class the name of the film you are going to present;
- give copies of the synopsis to the class;
- allow the class enough time to read the synopsis;
- answer any questions the class may have about the synopsis;
- show your key scenes to the class. Each member of the group should show one scene.

Each group member should explain:

- what happens in your scene (brief explanations, please!)
- why you think the scene is important
- why you (or the group) chose the scene
- what the class should look for in terms of:
  - plot development
  - character development
  - design features (costumes, setting, etc.)
  - writing and acting.

Answer any questions the class may have about the film.

Photocopiable © Oxford University Press

7.5 Film viewing project

Students study important scenes from a film over several lessons.

LEVEL

Intermediate and above

TIME

As many lessons as you wish to use

MATERIALS

A full-length feature film; a 'film' synopsis and a series of 'interim' synopses (see below).

PREPARATION

1 Watch the whole film yourself and divide it up into a number of dramatic scenes. These should include the beginning and the end, and a number of other scenes. Each individual scene should be no more than five or six minutes long.

2 Prepare a one-page, English-language synopsis of the film written at the students' level.

3 Prepare a series of one-paragraph 'interim' synopses, each on separate sheets, of what goes on between each of the scenes you have selected.

4 For each scene you have chosen, prepare a worksheet (or choose appropriate activities from this book) with general and more detailed comprehension questions and some follow-up communication activities.

PROCEDURE

Lesson 1

1 Prepare the students for the film-viewing project by distributing the film synopsis and going through it with them.

2 Play the opening credits and the first scene of the film. Discuss the scene with the class, and go through any useful language.

3 Play the scene again, and get students to predict what will happen next in the film. Remember not to rob the scene or the film of its drama and suspense.

4 Play the opening scene once more to consolidate the students' knowledge. This third time is the point where you might concentrate on the art of making the film, rather than on plot, character, and language. You might ask students to comment on the use of music or sound effects, or on the value of having some visual action behind the title, and you might choose to pause the video at one or two significant moments. Remember that understanding should increase enjoyment, not kill it.

5 Distribute the 'interim' synopsis you have prepared for this session. Ask students to read the synopsis before the next class session.

Other lessons

1 Ask the class questions to check that students have read and understood the 'interim' synopsis. Ask if their predictions about what happens have changed since reading the synopsis.

2 Introduce the next scene with some comprehension questions.

3 Play the scene. Get the class to answer the comprehension questions and discuss the scene.

4 Replay the scene and go through it in detail, explaining and practising key language used on the soundtrack. Use the PAUSE or STILL control buttons on the VCR to stop the action while you discuss each point.

5 If you have enough time, get students to act out or role-play part of the scene, give their opinions on the action, the characters, or the setting, and predict what will follow.

6 Distribute the appropriate 'interim' synopsis and ask students to read it before the next lesson.

Last lesson

This proceeds as previous lessons, but the students should be able to summarize what they liked and didn't like about the film. This could take the form of an informal whole-class discussion, or a more formal debate or panel discussion.

FOLLOW-UP

As a follow-up to viewing a film this way, you can ask students to carry out some of the activities in chapter 4, *Responding to whole films.*

VARIATION 1

Instead of showing just important scenes, you could break up the entire film into as many segments as you wish and show the entire film over a longer series of lessons. For this variation, you will not need to create the 'interim' synopses.

REMARKS

The preparation stage of this activity involves a lot of work, but once you have done it, the materials will be available for you and your colleagues to use and re-use as often as you choose.

Dealing with a film in this way satisfies the constraints of classroom timetables that limit individual class meetings to forty minutes or so. If the film-viewing project has been successful, students will want to watch the entire film straight through. If at all possible, try to allow for an afternoon or evening of extra-curricular activity where this can happen.

7.6 Make a movie magazine

Students make a collection of film-related materials they have created and organize it in the form of a magazine. Suitable film-related materials are produced by the students in activities such as 'Best film survey' (1.2), 'Character posters' (6.3), 'Dear film friend' (6.7), 'Design the remake' (3.2), 'Film memorabilia (3.5), 'Film posters' (1.7), 'Storyboards' (3.8), 'Writing film reviews' (4.5), and 'Writing film scripts' (3.9).

LEVEL

Elementary and above

TIME

As much time as you wish to spend on it.

MATERIALS

Sheets of paper (A4 or business-letter size), on which the finished work can be mounted. These sheets can then be photocopied or compiled into a class magazine.

PROCEDURE

1 Pieces of work produced by the students can be collected as students work on them, or you can spend several lessons collecting the work together and arranging it attractively. You work as editor, correcting the work as much as appropriate, and making the final decisions about what to include in the magazine.

2 To give the students ideas on content and style, show the class some examples of movie magazines. Point out examples of:

- content and style
- headlines
- captions for photos
- list of contents.

3 Ask the students to draw up a list of the contributors (everyone in the class). If possible, get them to include a photo or drawing of each contributor next to their name.

4 Together with the class, decide on the design and layout of the magazine. You can spend time in class designing a front and back cover, or assign the task for homework after discussing it in class. The class can vote on the best cover for the magazine.

5 If possible, have the magazine photocopied so that each student will have a personal copy. Keep in mind that photographs do not usually copy very well. A light setting on the photocopier gives the best results.

VARIATION

In higher-level classes you can divide the class into groups, and each group can work together to create their own magazine, using examples of their own work. You can suggest appropriate items to include.

Items that might be included

You may like to include letters from fans written to film stars asking questions about their lives and professional careers, responses from the film stars, film star profiles listing name, age, star sign, favourite colour, favourite animal, and so on, and word puzzles based on words related to films, the film industry, and film stars.

7.7 Make your own trailer

Students use extracts from a film to create a proposal for a trailer.

LEVEL

Intermediate and above

TIME

Two lessons of about 50 minutes

MATERIALS

A film that the students have studied or know well; a video of a theatrical **trailer**; blank overhead transparencies; transparency pens.

PREPARATION

The students should all have seen the same film; cue a copy of the film and the trailer.

PROCEDURE

Lesson 1

1 Divide the class into groups of four or five, and distribute blank overhead transparencies and transparency pens to each group.

2 Set up the following roleplay situation:

Each group is a **post-production company** specializing in trailers. You, the teacher, are the Head of Publicity for the production company which made the film that the students have studied. Each post-production company must prepare a proposal for the trailer. They must design a trailer for the film and create a storyboard illustrating their ideas. The best proposal will get the commission. There is a time limit on the proposal. Each proposal must be ready for presentation in the next lesson. Each post-production company will have five minutes to present a proposal for a trailer lasting 30–40 seconds.

3 Each group gives itself a name, for example, 'Flashfire Post-production'.

4 Each group:
- decides on the key 'selling points' of the film
- selects the extracts to be used

- writes a script for the trailer
- decides on the wording and design of the 'captions' to be put on the screen.

5 Each group prepares its presentation on overhead transparencies, and gets ready to cue the film to the extracts they want to use.

Lesson 2

6 Each post-production company introduces itself to the 'client' (the teacher) and makes its presentation. At the end of each presentation, the 'client' and the class have two minutes to ask questions.

7 After all the groups have done their presentations, 'the client' decides who will get the contract. The class discuss what they have learnt from the roleplay about:

- producing a trailer
- preparing and making a presentation.

Appendices

Appendix A Glossary of film terms

A-list star
A very popular film actor whose name on a new film guarantees a large number of people will come to see the film when it opens, e.g. Meg Ryan or Nicholas Cage.

Academy Awards
Merit prizes given annually since 1927 by the American Academy of Motion Picture Arts and Sciences. Prizes are awarded in 23 different categories, including Best Picture, Best Actor in a Leading Role, Best Actress in a Leading Role, and **Cinematography.**

action
Any movement in front of the camera.

boom
(1) a long 'arm' carrying a microphone to be balanced over the actors so that sound can be picked up; (2) a camera movement up or down through space; (3) a high movable platform that can support an entire camera unit.

closed-captioned
Accompanied by captions (printed versions of the dialogue) that can be seen only a specially equipped receiver: *closed-captioned films for the hearing-impaired.*

cast
(1) noun, the group of actors who perform in a film; (2) verb, to select an actor for a role.

character
A person in a book, play, or film.

cinematographer
The person who is responsible for the camerawork of a film.

cinematography
Motion picture photography.

clip
A short piece of a film, shown separately.

close-up
A **shot** of one face or object taken at close range and that fills the screen completely.

crew
The people who are involved with the production of a film and who do not appear in the film. The term is usually used to refer to the more subordinate members of a production team, in contrast to the **filmmakers.**

cut
(1) an abrupt transition from one **shot** to another, the first being immediately replaced by the second; (2) to **edit** a film, or (during filming) to stop the camera running on a scene.

dialogue
The words that the characters say in a film.

director
The person who supervises the creative aspects of a film and instructs the actors and **crew.**

dissolve	A gradual change of **scene**, in which the end of one scene is superimposed over the beginning of a new one.
documentary	A non-fiction film or television narrative without actors. Typically a documentary is a journalistic record of an event, person, or place.
dolly	A small platform that runs over railway-like tracks for the camera to follow the motion of the actors in a smooth fashion.
dub	To insert a new **soundtrack** on a film so that the dialogue is spoken by actors using a different language: *to dub a film in English.*
edit	To assemble a complete film from its various **shots** and **soundtracks**.
editor	The person who selects what they consider the best takes and pieces them together to produce a scene. The **editor** pieces the scenes into a sequence, which becomes the final film.
establishing shot	A **shot** that comes at the beginning of a **sequence** and that shows the audience the general location of the scene that follows, often providing essential information, and orienting the viewer.
extreme close-up	A **shot** of a small object or part of a face that fills the screen.
eye level	A **shot** that approximates human vision and in which the line between the camera and the subject being filmed is parallel to the ground.
fade out/fade in	A film editing technique in which one **scene** gradually goes dark and a new one gradually emerges from the darkness.
filmmaker	A person who has a significant degree of control over the creation of a film, e.g. a **director, producer,** or **editor.**
flashback	A **sequence** of a film that goes back in time to show what happened earlier in the story.
frame	A single picture image that eventually appears on the **print** of a film.
freeze-frame	A still picture from a videotape, made by using the pause button.
genre	A type or class of film, e.g. horror film, comedy, musical, western, etc.
high angle	A **shot** in which the camera looks down on what is being filmed.
intercut	The act of cutting from one **shot** to the next to show **characters** as they engage in **dialogue**.
interior monologue	A passage of writing presenting a character's inner thoughts and emotions.
lead	The main or most important **character** in a film.
level camera angle	An angle in which the camera lens is even with the subject.
lip-synching	The matching of lip movements with recorded speech.
literary elements	Features that films share with literature, e.g. **plot, characters, setting, point of view, mood,** and **theme.**

long shot	A **shot** taken from enough distance to show a landscape, a building, or a large crowd.
low angle	A **shot** in which the camera looks up at what is being filmed.
medium shot	A **shot** between a long shot and a close-up that might show two people in full figure or several people from the waist up.
minor role	A small part in a film.
mood	The general impression that a film gives to the viewer.
opening shot	A **shot** used at the beginning a film.
Oscar	The affectionate name given to the statuette that is given to Academy Award winners.
Oscar ceremony	The annual Academy Awards ceremony held in Los Angeles, California. Sometimes called *the Oscars*.
outtake	A piece of film that is not being used at the time, but is saved in case it may be needed for use at a later date.
pan	A **shot** in which the camera rotates horizontally to the left (**pan left**) or right (**pan right**). Also used as a verb.
plot	The main story-line of a film.
point of view	(1) a camera **shot** that shows audiences how a scene looks from one character's position in the scene; (2) the attitude or outlook of a narrator or character in a piece of literature or a film. (Please note that the definition of this term 'point of view' has been expanded to reflect its use in 2.13, 'Talk about the story'.)
post-production company	A firm that is associated with doing work on a film after the **principal filming** has been completed.
portray	To act the part of a particular **character** in a film.
principal photography	The filming of the major components of a film.
print	A copy of a film.
problem	A difficult situation, matter or person that a **character** or characters has to deal with or think about.
producer	The person who initiates the creation of the film. The **producer** finds the script, hires a director, finds financing and a studio to back the film, and markets the film.
remake	A new version of an old film.
role	An actor's part in a film.
scene	A series of **shots** that take place in a single location or are part of the same general action. See also **sequence.**
screenplay	A written description of the **dialogue** and action of a film, often with basic camera directions. See also **script.**
script	A written description of the **dialogue** and action of a film, often with basic camera directions. See also **screenplay.**
scriptwriter	The person who writes the text for a film.

sequence	A series of **scenes** unified by a shared action.
setting	The time, place, and circumstances in which the action of a film takes place.
shot	A unit of film in which the camera does not stop filming.
solution	The way a **character** or characters solve a problem or deal with a difficult situation.
sound effects	Imitative sounds (e.g. of thunder or an explosion) that are produced artificially for a film.
soundtrack	(1) all the recorded sound of a film, including **dialogue, sound effects**, and music; (2) the music that accompanies a film.
special effects	A general term that covers many tricks of filmmaking that cannot be achieved by direct photography.
star	An actor who is famous for playing important parts in popular films.
still	A photograph of a **shot** from a film.
storyboard	A series of drawings showing the **scenes, shot** by shot, and transitions for a film. The storyboard gives the **director** a clear idea of how the final film will look.
strap line	(Called a **tag line** in the U.S.) an advertising line written underneath the main title of a film, e.g 'You'll believe a Man Can Fly!' for the film *Superman: The Movie* (1978).
subtext	The hidden meanings in a conversation, not expressed by words, but other means such as intonation, tone of voice, timing, facial expression, gesture, eye contact, and posture.
subtitle	A printed translation of the **dialogue** of a foreign-language film shown at the bottom of the screen, e.g. a French film with English *subtitles*.
synopsis	A short description of the main parts of a story.
theatrical trailer	A **trailer** that is shown in a cinema before the main feature film.
theme	A general subject, topic, or message that runs throughout a film.
tilt	A **shot** in which the camera points up (**tilt up**) or down (**tilt down**) from a fixed base.
title	The name given to a film.
title sequence	The written material displayed on the screen at the beginning of a film for the audience to read, and giving the names of the people involved in the production of the film (e.g. the main actors, director, producer, etc.). Sometimes called *opening credits* or *titles*.
tracking shot	A **shot** taken with a moving camera, usually forward or backward, and sometimes on an actual track.
trailer	A short filmed advertisement for a feature film. It uses highlights from the film with graphics and voice-over commentary to publicise the film. See also **theatrical trailer.**

transcript	A written copy of the dialogue that is spoken in a film. Unlike the **screenplay** of a film, which is written before the film is produced and which is meant to serve as a guide to making the film, a transcript is a written record of the dialogue that actually appears on the *soundtrack* of the film.
treatment	A written summary of a proposed film. It covers the basic ideas and issues of the film: story, main **characters**, locations, and story.
underscoring	The music on the **soundtrack** of a film.
voice-over	The voice of a narrator, generally not seen, heard on a **soundtrack** of a film.
wipe	A device used for quick changes of scene: a line appears at an edge or corner of the screen and 'wipes' across, bringing a new picture with it.
zoom	The use of the camera lens to move closer to (**zoom in**) or farther from (**zoom out**) the subject being filmed.

Appendix B Internet resources for film

The Internet offers many film-related websites. We present here a brief list of some useful links that can help teachers who want to plan lessons based on feature films.

The Internet is constantly changing; inclusion in this list does not necessarily mean that the authors or publishers of this book endorse either these sites or their content.

All-Movie Guide

http://allmovie.com/

A film and video directory with reviews and synopses.

Ari Rukkila's Motion Picture Screenplay Links

http://www.kolumbus.fi/rukkila/scripts.htm

Links to over 150 screenplays, from *Apocalypse Now* to *Young Frankenstein.*

Drew's Scripts-O-Rama

http://www.script-o-rama.com/

A comprehensive collection of scripts and transcripts of feature films.

Empire Magazine

http://www.empireonline.co.uk

News, features, and reviews of every film showing in the UK.

ESL Cafe's Cinema Forum

http://www.eslcafe.com/discussion/da

An interactive forum where learners of English can discuss films.

Film Critic Homepage

http://www.filmcritic.com/

Links to reviews and plot summaries of popular films.

Filmfinder.com

http://www.filmfinder.com/

Information about where to buy videos of feature films you are looking for, and where and when you can see a particular film on television or in a cinema.

Film SL

http://www.latrobe.edu.au/www/education/sl/sl.html

Information on how to join a discussion list for learners of English who are interested in cinema.

Movie Talk

http://www.elfs.com/moviesEnt.html

Website where students can write their opinions of films they have seen.

The Movie Times: Top 100 Films Ever Worldwide

http://www.the-movie-times.com/thrsdir/top100world.html

A list of the best 100 films ever made.

The Movie Turf

http://www.geocities.com/Hollywood/9371/scriptlist1.htm

Links to over 450 screenplays, film transcripts, reviews, and soundtracks.

Movie Web: Top 50 All Time Highest Grossing Movies

http://www.movieweb.com/movie/alltime.html

A list of films which have made the most money ever.

The Greatest Films of All Time

http://www.filmsite.org/films.html

Links to background information, plot summaries, and reviews of more than 150 films, images of classic film posters, an extensive film bibliography, and more.

The Internet Film Database

http://us.imdb.org/

A comprehensive database with links to plot summaries, film reviews, film trivia, biographies, filmographies, film quotes, trailers, and other resources.

Oscar.com

http://www.oscar.com

Website with trivia quizzes, best picture posters, Academy Award history, lists of past Oscar winners, and an Academy Award database where you can search for any nominee and get their Oscar history.

Scott Renshaw: 100 Top Grossing Films of All Time

http://inconnect.com/~renshaw/topgross.html

A list of the 100 films that have made the most money ever.

Screen Network Australia

http://www.sna.net.au

A gateway to Australian film sites.

Yahoo! Entertainment: Movies

http://dir.yahoo.com/Entertainment/Movies_and_Film/
A starting place leading to hundreds of film sites.

Yahoo! Entertainment: Screenplays

http://dir.yahoo.com/Entertainment/Movies_and_Film/Screenplays/
Links to screenplays.

Appendix C Video troubleshooting guide

Here is a simple video troubleshooting guide for your video player
(VCR) and monitor.

Problem	Check
No power	VCR and TV plugged in?
	Mains switched on?
	VCR and TV switched on?
No picture	Monitor switched on?
	Video lead/cable connected?
	AV button pressed?
	Monitor correctly tuned to video?
	Brightness control too low?
	Video channel selected?
	Video standard compatible with equipment? (See Appendix D, 'International TV standards for video', on page 151)
	Video on standby? (Press standby to reactivate or turn monitor off and then on again.)
No sound	Volume control too low?
	'Mute' button active?
	Sound lead/cable connected?
Interference	Adjust tracking?
	Adjust tuning?
	Video standard compatible with equipment?
Unwanted sound	Incorrect tuning?
	Monitor ' slipped off' video channel?
No response from switches	Turn off timer button?
	Is 'operate' switch on?

Videocassette won't insert   Remove other videocassette?

Turn off timer button?

Videocassette compatible with system?

DVD problems

The same problems as occur for video can occur for DVD, but note that DVDs are formatted for particular worldwide regions and unless the player contains a special chip, videos formatted for one region will not play in another. See Appendix E, 'DVD worldwide regions', on page 154 for a list of DVD regions and the geographical areas they cover.

Appendix D International TV standards for video

Videotapes for foreign countries need to conform to local standards to insure compatibility. Here is a listing of TV standards used around the world.

Country	System	Country	System
Afghanistan	PAL	Costa Rica	NTSC
Albania	PAL	Cuba	NTSC
Algeria	PAL	Cyprus	PAL
Angola	PAL	Czech Republic	SECAM
Argentina	PAL	Dahomey	SECAM
Australia	PAL	Denmark	PAL
Austria	PAL	Djibouti	SECAM
Azerbaijan	SECAM	Dominican Republic	NTSC
Azores	PAL	Ecuador	NTSC
Bahamas	NTSC	Egypt	SECAM
Bahrain	PAL	Equatorial Guinea	PAL
Bangladesh	PAL	El Salvador	NTSC
Barbados	NTSC	Ethiopia	PAL
Belgium	PAL	Fiji	PAL
Bermuda	NTSC	Finland	PAL
Bolivia	NTSC	France	SECAM
Botswana	PAL	French Polynesia	SECAM
Brazil	PAL	Gabon	SECAM
Bulgaria	SECAM	Gambia	PAL
Burkina Faso	SECAM	Germany	PAL
Burma-Myanmar	NTSC	Ghana	PAL
Cambodia	NTSC	Gibraltar	PAL
Cameroon	PAL	Greece	PAL
Canada	NTSC	Greenland	NTSC/PAL
Canary Islands	PAL	Guadeloupe	SECAM
Chad	SECAM	Guam	NTSC
Chile	NTSC	Guatemala	NTSC
China	PAL	Guyana	SECAM
Colombia	NTSC	Guinea	PAL
Congo	SECAM	Honduras	NTSC

Hong Kong	PAL	Nepal	PAL
Hungary	SECAM/ PAL	Netherlands	PAL
		Netherlands Antilles	NTSC
Iceland	PAL		
India	PAL	New Caledonia	SECAM
Indonesia	PAL	New Guinea	PAL
Iran	SECAM	New Zealand	PAL
Iraq	SECAM	Nicaragua	NTSC
Ireland	PAL	Niger	SECAM
Israel	PAL	Nigeria	PAL
Italy	PAL	Norway	PAL
Ivory Coast	SECAM	Oman	PAL
Jamaica	NTSC	Pakistan	PAL
Japan	NTSC	Panama	NTSC
Jordan	PAL	Paraguay	PAL
Kenya	PAL	Peru	NTSC
Korea (North)	SECAM	Philippines	NTSC
Korea (South)	NTSC	Poland	SECAM
Kuwait	PAL	Portugal	PAL
Lebanon	SECAM	Puerto Rico	NTSC
Liberia	PAL	Qatar	PAL
Libya	SECAM	Reunion	SECAM
Luxembourg	PAL	Romania	PAL
Madagascar	SECAM	Russia	SECAM
Madeira	PAL	Rwanda	SECAM
Malagasy	SECAM	Sabah/Sarawak	PAL
Malawi	PAL	Saint Kitts	NTSC
Malaysia	PAL	Samoa	NTSC
Mali	SECAM	Saudi Arabia	SECAM/PAL
Malta	PAL	Senegal	SECAM
Martinique	SECAM	Seychelles	PAL
Mauritania	SECAM	Sierra Leone	PAL
Mauritius	SECAM	Singapore	PAL
Mexico	NTSC	Slovakia	PAL
Monaco	SECAM	Somalia	PAL
Mongolia	SECAM	South Africa	PAL
Morocco	SECAM	Spain	PAL
Mozambique	PAL	Sri Lanka	PAL
Namibia	PAL	Sudan	PAL

Surinam	NTSC	Uganda	PAL
Swaziland	PAL	United Arab Emirates	PAL
Sweden	PAL	United Kingdom	PAL
Switzerland	PAL	United States	NTSC
Syria	SECAM	Upper Volta	SECAM
Tahiti	SECAM	Uruguay	PAL
Taiwan	NTSC	Venezuela	NTSC
Tanzania	PAL	Vietnam	PAL
Thailand	PAL	Yemen	PAL
Togo	SECAM	Yugoslavia	PAL
Trinidad and Tobago	NTSC	Zaire	SECAM
Tunisia	SECAM	Zambia	PAL
Turkey	PAL	Zimbabwe	PAL

Appendix E DVD worldwide regions

Like videotapes, DVDs for foreign countries need to conform to local standards to insure compatibility. The publishers of DVDs have established a system of worldwide regions. Here is a listing of the regions and the areas they cover.

Region 1	USA, Canada
Region 2	Europe, Near East, South Africa, Japan
Region 3	South East Asia
Region 4	Australia, Central and South America
Region 5	Africa, Asia, Eastern Europe
Region 6	China

Bibliography

Aycock, W. and M. Schoenecke (eds.). 1988. *Film and Literature: A comparative approach to adaptation*. Lubbock, TX: Texas Tech University Press.

Baddock, B. 1996. *Using Films in the English Class*. Hemel Hempstead: Phoenix ELT.

Bone, J. and R. Johnson. 1997. *Understanding the Film: An introduction to film appreciation*. Lincolnwood, IL: NTC Publishing Group.

Costanzo, W.B. 1992. *Reading the Films: Twelve great films on video and how to teach them*. Urbana, IL: National Council of Teachers of English.

Geddes, M. and G. Sturtridge. (eds.) 1982 *Video in the Language Classroom*. London: Heinemann Educational Books.

Holden, A. 1994. *The Oscars, the Secret History of Hollywood's Academy Awards*. Warner Books.

Lacey, R.A. 1972. *Seeing with Feeling: Film in the classroom*. Philadelphia and London: W. B. Saunders Company.

Lloyd-Kolkin, D. and K. R. Tyner 1991. *Media and You*. Englewood Cliffs, NJ: Educational Technology Publications.

Meinhof, U.H. 1998. *Language Learning in the Age of Satellite Television*. Oxford: Oxford University Press.

Mejia, E., M.K. Xiao and J. Kennedy. 1994. *102 Very Teachable Films*. Englewood Cliffs, NJ. Prentice Hall Regents.

Moskowitz, G. 1978. *Caring and Sharing in the Language Class*. Rowley, MA: Newbury House Publishers.

Resch, K.E. and V.D. Schicker. 1992. *Using Film in the High School Curriculum: A practical guide for teachers and librarians*. Jefferson, NC and London: McFarland & Company.

Stempleski, S. and P. Arcario (eds.). 1992. *Video in Second Language Teaching: Using, selecting and producing video for the classroom*. Alexandria, VA: Teachers of English to Speakers of Other Languages.

Stempleski, S. and B. Tomalin. 1990. *Video in Action: Recipes for using video in language teaching*. New York and London: Prentice Hall.

Summerfield, E. 1993. *Crossing Cultures through Film*. Yarmouth, ME: Intercultural Press.

Teasley, A. B. and A. Wilder. 1996. *Reel Conversations: Reading films with young adults*. Portsmouth, NH: Heinemann.

Tomalin, B. 2000. *Teaching English with Technology*. Chelmsford, Essex: IBI Multimedia.

Tomalin, B. and S. Stempleski. 1993. *Cultural Awareness*. Oxford: Oxford University Press.

Other titles in the Resource Books for Teachers series

Beginners, by Peter Grundy—communicative activities for both absolute and 'false' beginners, including those who do not know the Roman alphabet. All ages. (ISBN 0 19 437200 6)

Class Readers, by Jean Greenwood—activities to develop extensive and intensive reading skills, plus listening and speaking tasks. All ages. (ISBN 0 19 437103 4)

Classroom Dynamics, by Jill Hadfield—helps teachers maintain a good working relationship with their classes, and so promote effective learning. Teenagers and adults. (ISBN 0 19 437147 6)

Conversation, by Rob Nolasco and Lois Arthur—over 80 activities to develop students' ability to speak confidently and fluently. Teenagers and adults. (ISBN 0 19 437096 8)

Creating Stories with Children, by Andrew Wright—encourages creativity, confidence, and fluency and accuracy in spoken and written English. Age 7–14. (ISBN 0 19 437204 9)

Cultural Awareness, by Barry Tomalin and Susan Stempleski— challenges stereotypes, using cultural issues as a rich resource for language practice. Teenagers and adults. (ISBN 0 19 437194 8)

Dictionaries, by Jonathan Wright—ideas for making more effective use of dictionaries in class. Teenagers and adults. (ISBN 019 437219 7)

Drama, by Charlyn Wessels—creative and enjoyable activities using drama to teach spoken communication skills and literature. Teenagers and adults. (ISBN 0 19 437097 6)

Drama with Children, by Sarah Phillips—practical ideas to develop speaking skills, self-confidence, imagination, and creativity. Age 6–12. (ISBN 0 19 437220 0)

Exam Classes, by Peter May—preparation for a wide variety of public examinations, including most of the main American and British exams. Teenagers and adults. (ISBN 0 19 437208 1)

Games for Children, by Gordon Lewis with GŸnther Bedson—an exciting collection of games for children aged 4 to 12. (ISBN 0 19 437224 3)

Grammar Dictation, by Ruth Wajnryb—the 'dictogloss'

technique—improves understanding and use of grammar by reconstructing texts. Teenagers and adults. (ISBN 0 19 437004 6)

The Internet, by Scott Windeatt, David Hardisty, and David Eastment—motivates learners and brings a wealth of material into the classroom. For all levels of expertise. Teenagers and adults. (ISBN 0 19 437223 5)

Learner-based Teaching, by Colin Campbell and Hanna Kryszewska—unlocks the wealth of knowledge that learners bring to the classroom. All ages. (ISBN 0 19 437163 8)

Letters, by Nicky Burbidge, Peta Gray, Sheila Levy, and Mario Rinvolucri—using letters and e-mail for language and cultural study. Teenagers and adults. (ISBN 0 19 442149 X)

Listening, by Goodith White—advice and ideas for encouraging learners to become 'active listeners'. Teenagers and adults. (ISBN 0 19 437216 2)

Literature, by Alan Maley and Alan Duff—an innovatory book on using literature for language practice. Teenagers and adults. (ISBN 0 19 437094 1)

Music and Song, by Tim Murphey—'tuning in' to students' musical tastes can increase motivation and tap a rich vein of resources. All ages. (ISBN 0 19 437055 0)

Newspapers, by Peter Grundy—original ideas for making effective use of newspapers in lessons. Teenagers and adults. (ISBN 0 19 437192 6)

Projects with Young Learners, by Diane Phillips, Sarah Burwood, and Helen Dunford—encourages learner independence by producing a real sense of achievement. Age 5 to 13. (ISBN 0 19 437221 9)

Project Work, by Diana L. Fried-Booth—bridges the gap between the classroom and the outside world. Teenagers and adults. (ISBN 0 19 437092 5)

Pronunciation, by Clement Laroy—imaginative activities to build confidence and improve all aspects of pronunciation. All ages. (ISBN 0 19 437087 9)

Role Play, by Gillian Porter Ladousse—controlled conversations to improvised drama, simple dialogues to complex scenarios. Teenagers and adults. (ISBN 0 19 437095 X)

Self-Access, by Susan Sheerin—advice on setting up and managing self-access study facilities, plus materials. Teenagers and adults. (ISBN 0 19 437099 2)

Storytelling with Children, by Andrew Wright—hundreds of exciting ideas for using stories to teach English to children aged 7 to 14. (ISBN 0 19 437202 2)

Translation, by Alan Duff—a wide variety of translation activities from many different subject areas. Teenagers and adults. (ISBN 0 19 437104 2)

Very Young Learners, by Vanessa Reilly and Sheila M. Ward— advice and ideas for teaching children aged 3 to 6 years, including games, songs, drama, stories, and art and crafts. (ISBN 0 19 437209 X)

Video, by Richard Cooper, Mike Lavery, and Mario Rinvolucri— original ideas for watching and making videos. All ages. (ISBN 0 19 437102 6)

Vocabulary, by John Morgan and Mario Rinvolucri—a wide variety of communicative activities for teaching new words. Teenagers and adults. (ISBN 019 437091 7)

Writing, by Tricia Hedge—a wide range of writing tasks, as well as guidance on student difficulties with writing. Teenagers and adults. (ISBN 0 19 437098 4)

Young Learners, by Sarah Phillips—advice and ideas for teaching English to children aged 6–12, including arts and crafts, games, stories, poems, and songs. (ISBN 0 19 437195 6)

Index

Numbers in *Italics* refer to items in the introductory sections and glossary (which are marked *g*).